onewith**christ**.com

CONE WITH CHRIST

A Bible Study Series

SERIES ONE

Faith and Reality

G B Woodcock

Now to the King eternal,

immortal,

invisible,

the only God,

be honor and glory

forever and ever.

Amen.

English definitions of Greek and Hebrew words are taken from:
- *Online Bible Greek Lexicon* © 2010 Online Bible North America. All rights reserved.
- *Online Bible Hebrew Lexicon* © 2010 Online Bible North America. All rights
  reserved.

Unless otherwise stated, all Scripture quotations are taken from:
The *New American Standard Bible* ® (1995 Update) Copyright ©1960, 1962, 1963, 1968, 1971, 1972, 1973, 1975, 1977, 1995 by the Lockman Foundation. Used by permission. All rights reserved.

Scripture quotations marked (NKJV) are taken from the *New King James Version,* ©1979, 1980, 1982 by Thomas Nelson, Inc. Used by permission. All rights reserved.

Scripture quotations marked (NRSV) are taken from the *New Revised Standard Version* Bible, © 1989 by the division of Christian Education of the National Council of the churches of Christ in the U.S.A. Used by permission. All rights reserved.

Scripture quotations marked (Amplified Version) are taken from the *Amplified Bible,* Copyright © 1954, 1958, 1962, 1964, 1965, 1987 by The Lockman Foundation. Used by permission.

One with Christ | **Series One** - *G B Woodcock*
A Bible study series on experiencing love and unity with God

Web | www.onewithchrist.com
Email | info@onewithchrist.com

ISBN: 978-0-9864695-2-7

Published by Studyword Media
Printed in the United States of America

Contents

Introduction

My heart stands in awe of Your word.
I rejoice at Your word as one who finds great treasure.
Psalm 119:161b-162 (NKJV)

The living word of God has the power to leave our hearts in awe. It is like great treasure, revealing to us the riches that are found in the life, presence and love of Jesus. But how do we find the riches of Christ? How does the knowledge of spiritual wealth and abundance become our actual experience?

Life in Christ is not based on a set of theories or theologies. Life in Jesus is found in the reality of a living relationship. As such, if we are to grow and mature in Christ then we need our knowledge of the truth to be completed by real experience. For example, we can know the theory about God's love, but without the experience of His love in our lives, all we have is a theory or idea. And theory is not reality. The only way to know the reality of God's love is to personally experience His love. In this way, experiencing God is a key aspect of living and growing in Christ.

Spirit and Life

As we grow in Christ, we will go through different spiritual seasons. In these seasons God will do His work in us, leading us to experience different aspects of His life and nature. If we are to stay in step with the Spirit as He works in us, then we need to focus on what God is doing now. Anything, no matter how good, can be a distraction if it is not in His timing. This includes these studies: they will only be helpful if the Spirit of God is actively working through them. So how can we know if God wants to use the *One with Christ* studies at this time?

The words of Jesus are spirit and life.[1] This is a basic but essential truth on which we can stand. If the Spirit of God is working through something, there will be a sense of life and freedom in it. So in terms of the *One with Christ* studies, if you find life in the studies, feel free to dive in and get as much life and blessing out of them as possible. However, if the studies are dry and lifeless, if they make no sense, are a struggle to read, or if they simply do not flow for you, then it is probably not the right time to do the studies. So leave them. Put the studies on the shelf and come back to them later when you find a sense of life in them. It may well be that God is doing something different in you at this time. So just seek God for what He is doing now. If He wants to use the *One with Christ* studies to draw you closer to Him, then He will bring you back to them when the time is right. Simply go where there is life.

Discovering More

As you do the studies, if you find a particular sense of life or enjoyment in any passage or study, feel free to take the study further. Read through the Scriptures in their entire context. Explore more of God's word by finding related passages and see what the Spirit of God shows you personally from His word. As you study, remember that our goal is not just to build our knowledge of the truth, but to enter into and live in the reality of the truth. So as we learn more in the word, we need to seek God to lead us into the personal experience of His truth. As He leads us, we grow closer to Jesus and become more connected with Him.

It is important to realize that God shows different aspects of a truth to different people and this series does not claim to reveal the whole of any one truth. There is always more to learn and discover. These studies simply aim to offer a fresh perspective of Scripture with the hope that you would take hold of the truth and experience some of the awesome depths of Christ in your life.

Solid Foundations

The first few studies lay a foundation of reality. The next studies look at our inheritance in Christ and how we can go deeper into the life that He has for us. The studies following those focus on faith.

So what do all these things have to do with becoming one with Christ? What does it mean to be one with Christ?

One with Christ

1 Corinthians 6:17
But the one who joins himself to the Lord is one spirit with Him.

The term *One with Christ* comes from this Scripture. When we join ourselves to the Lord, we become one spirit with Him. Thus it is a promise of God that when we connect ourselves deeply and intimately with Him, we will become one spirit with Him. It is certainly one of the mysteries of God, but a promise and a reality nonetheless. We can become one with Christ.

Having unity with God as our goal, *Series One* starts by building a foundation of faith. It establishes an understanding of growth and experience, and how the Spirit and the word work together to draw us into reality. *Series Two* then builds on this foundation and looks more at becoming one with Christ. Thus doing the studies in order is advised to gain the most benefit from the series. However, as with all things, let the Spirit lead you as you study His word.

My prayer is that you would grow in love, faith, life and truth as you do these studies. May God bring you to a point of abundantly overflowing in these things. May He be faithful to His word and lead you into the reality of all He has prepared for you.

Author, *One with Christ*

Study 1

Ω

Truth and Reality

Buy truth and do not sell it, get wisdom and
instruction and understanding.
Proverbs 23:23

Scripture calls us to buy the truth and hold on to it. As we
mature in our spiritual life, we grow in the truth that is found
in Christ. But what is truth? And having come to know the
truth, how do we experience it in our lives?

What is Truth?

Truth: *aletheia*

Denotes veracity, reality, sincerity, accuracy,
integrity, truthfulness, dependability, and
propriety. Is the opposite of fictitious, feigned,
or false.

In early Greek culture, the word *aletheia* was used to express reality as opposed to fantasy or illusion.[1] In this sense, truth *is* reality. So to gain a deeper understanding of truth, we can look at what Scripture says of truth in terms of reality.

The Word

John 17:13-17

"But now I come to You; and these things I speak in the world so that they may have My joy made full in themselves. I have given them Your word; and the world has hated them, because they are not of the world, even as I am not of the world. I do not ask You to take them out of the world, but to keep them from the evil one. They are not of the world, even as I am not of the world. Sanctify them in the truth; Your word is truth."

The word of God is truth. It is the written expression of reality. The Scriptures reveal the truth of Jesus and describe the experiences that we can have as we grow in Christ.

For example, the word describes the truth of forgiveness. It reveals the forgiving nature of God and the reality of Christ's sacrifice for our sins. The word then shows us how to receive the forgiveness of God. When we follow its instruction and we repent and call on God in faith, we experience the reality of being forgiven. In this way, the truth of the word builds a foundation for our experience in Christ.

Jesus Christ

John 14:6
Jesus said to him, "I am the way, and the truth, and the life; no one comes to the Father but through Me."

Jesus is the truth. All reality flows from Jesus because He is the ultimate reality. He is also the way. It is only through Jesus that we can experience the reality of God and live in the truth. Thus if we want to know reality and life, we need Jesus.

Colossians 1:16-17
For by Him all things were created, both in the heavens and on earth, visible and invisible, whether thrones or dominions or rulers or authorities—all things have been created through Him and for Him. He is before all things, and in Him all things hold together.

Jesus is the creator and sustainer of all things. Things only exist because Jesus causes them to exist. He is reality and He makes things real. All things are made through Him and for Him. This means we are created not for ourselves, but for Christ, to live our lives in love with Him. Thus Jesus is the reason, meaning, goal and fulfillment of our lives.

To live in Christ means to live in reality, for He is reality. In this sense, to live apart from Jesus is to live apart from the truth, in a fantasy or false reality.

The Spirit

John 14:16-17

"I will ask the Father, and He will give you another Helper, that He may be with you forever; that is the Spirit of truth, whom the world cannot receive, because it does not see Him or know Him, but you know Him because He abides with you and will be in you."

John 16:13

"But when He, the Spirit of truth, comes, He will guide you into all the truth; for He will not speak on His own initiative, but whatever He hears, He will speak; and He will disclose to you what is to come."

1 John 5:6

This is the One who came by water and blood, Jesus Christ; not with the water only, but with the water and with the blood. It is the Spirit who testifies, because the Spirit is the truth.

The Spirit of God is the Spirit of truth and reality. God has sent the Spirit to abide in us, which means that He is always present to take us deeper into truth. It is the Spirit's role to lead us into reality and He has the power and desire to do it. *He wants to do it.* We simply need to yield to His will, His way and His timing to experience more of the reality of Jesus.

Our Reality

The word of God describes reality and Jesus has given us His Spirit to lead us into reality. In this way, God has given us everything we need to know and experience the truth. We have knowledge through the word and power by the Spirit.

Knowing that we have what we need to live in truth and reality, we can start by seeking to discover our present reality. Where are we spiritually? What are we currently experiencing of God?

> **Revelation 3:14-19**
> "To the angel of the church in Laodicea write: The Amen, the faithful and true Witness, the Beginning of the creation of God, says this: 'I know your deeds, that you are neither cold nor hot; I wish that you were cold or hot. So because you are lukewarm, and neither hot nor cold, I will spit you out of My mouth. Because you say, "I am rich, and have become wealthy, and have need of nothing," and you do not know that you are wretched and miserable and poor and blind and naked, I advise you to buy from Me gold refined by fire so that you may become rich, and white garments so that you may clothe yourself, and that the shame of your nakedness will not be revealed; and eye salve to anoint your eyes so that you may see. Those whom I love, I reprove and discipline; therefore be zealous and repent.'"

A key part of growing in the truth is learning who we are now and who we can actually become in Christ. Knowing our spiritual condition gives us a starting point in our spiritual growth. Knowing who we can become in Christ gives us a vision and goal for our growth.

The reality we live in is defined by our present experience. Yet like the Laodiceans, at times we can become out of touch with our own spiritual life. We can let our natural experience and the daily demands of life cloud our spiritual vision and desire for Jesus. We can start to believe the theory without seeking the reality. As a result, at times our perception of our spiritual state can become distorted. We can believe that we are doing well, when in reality we are spiritually poor, lacking the riches found in Jesus. Conversely, at times we may feel discouraged, thinking things are not going well, when in reality our spiritual life is better than we think. Thus a key part of knowing the truth is discovering the reality of our own spiritual condition.

Once the Spirit reveals the nature of our state before God, we can start to grow. Jesus will show us where He is taking us and what we need for our next step. If we are spiritually blind, He will offer us eye salve that we may see. If we are spiritually naked, He will offer us white garments. If we are poor, He will offer us His true wealth. Jesus will meet our need so that we can change, grow and live in the reality of the spiritual wealth of Christ.

So do we really want to know our current spiritual state? Do we want to live more in the truth of God?

Summary

Truth is reality and Jesus is the ultimate truth. He is the center and source of all reality. So to live more in the truth is to live in deeper connection and relationship with Jesus. It is to experience more of the life, love, nature, presence and power of Christ.

The word of God describes the reality that is found in Jesus. Because the word is truth, the experiences we have of God will always be consistent with the word. It is the standard of reality. It is the foundation for our spiritual experience.

God has given us His Spirit to lead us into reality. The Spirit of God takes the truth of the word and leads us into the personal experience of that truth. In this way the Spirit and the word work together to draw us into reality.

But how does all this really work? How does the Spirit work with the word? How does He lead us into all truth and reality? And is this something we really want?

Questions

What are the sources of truth in my life?

Where am I spiritually now? Where am I going?

How can I enter more into reality?

Study 2

February 3, 2014

Ⴕ

Spirit and Reality

"But when He, the Spirit of truth, comes,
He will guide you into all the truth."
John 16:13

Truth is reality. The word of God is truth and the role of the Spirit is to guide us into truth. But what does it actually mean to enter into truth and reality?

God is Spirit

> **John 4:24**
> "God is spirit, and those who worship Him must worship in spirit and truth."

God is Spirit and so our relationship with Him is primarily spiritual. Thus if we want to enter into reality then we need to look to our inner, spiritual growth in Jesus rather than our outward, natural life. The physical realm is not neglected, but it is secondary to the reality that is found in the Spirit. As such, our spiritual growth is of more value than our material wealth and needs to be given our highest priority.

> **2 Corinthians 4:16-18**
> Therefore we do not lose heart, but though our outer man is decaying, yet our inner man is being renewed day by day. For momentary, light affliction is producing for us an eternal weight of glory far beyond all comparison, while we look not at the things which are seen, but at the things which are not seen; for the things which are seen are temporal, but the things which are not seen are eternal.

The spiritual is more important than the physical and so spiritual realities are more important than physical realities. This is because the unseen spiritual is eternal and is therefore of eternal value. The physical however is temporal and only has passing value.

The eternal includes the present. Thus because spiritual realities are eternal, they are available for us to experience now. For example, peace is a reality that is eternally available; we can experience God's peace now. The same is true for all the qualities of God. His love, joy, passion, life, presence, strength, humility, wisdom, and zeal are all realities that are present and available to us now.

Spiritual Reality

Galatians 5:22-34

But the fruit of the Spirit is love, joy, peace, patience, kindness, goodness, faithfulness, gentleness, self-control; against such things there is no law.

The reality of each fruit of the Spirit is found in Jesus. Each quality is an aspect of His nature. So as we grow spiritually, we enter into more of the nature of Christ. For example, when we experience love, we experience Jesus for He is love.[1] As we enter into joy, we enter a deeper realm of Christ who is the source of joy.[2] As we grow in freedom and life, we grow in Christ for He is our freedom and life.[3] Every aspect of our spiritual life flows from Jesus. He is the reality.

So how do we experience these different qualities of Jesus?

Within our Hearts

Romans 5:5

...and hope does not disappoint, because the love of God has been poured out within our hearts through the Holy Spirit who was given to us.

As Scripture shows, we experience the love of God poured out in our hearts through His Spirit. The same is true for all the spiritual realities or qualities of God: we experience them in our hearts.

Heart: *kardia*

That organ in the animal body which is the center of the circulation of the blood, and hence was regarded as the seat of physical life; denotes the center of all physical and spiritual life; the vigor and sense of physical life; **the center and seat of spiritual life.**

In Scripture, the word *kardia* (heart) is almost entirely used in a spiritual sense, referring to the center of our spiritual life.[4] Thus the heart is a metaphor for the inner being of our spirit.[5] It is the center of our spiritual life and experience.[6] So when God pours out His love within us, it is a spiritual experience of the heart.

Without the spirit, we have no life. So just as our heart is the center of our spiritual life, it is also the underlying essence of our physical life. In this way, the effects of our spiritual experience are not confined to the heart. The love that we receive in our heart flows into our mind and body. It shapes our thinking and changes the way we feel in our body. The connection between our mind, body and spirit, means that our whole being is changed with our spiritual experience.

Often we can be tempted to associate the spiritual with the supernatural. However according to Scripture, our spiritual experiences should be as natural and common as love. Every day we can experience more of the reality of Jesus.

Concept to Reality

To enter into a spiritual reality is to personally experience the truth of the word in our hearts. If we know the word of God, then we have an intellectual knowledge of the truth. However real knowledge comes by experience. So for our intellectual knowledge to be of any value, it needs to be completed by personal experience. Our experience of truth is what matters.

For example, in the natural realm we can learn about the theory of swimming. We can study the theory of how to float on water and propel ourselves through the water. Yet in itself, our knowledge is only knowledge. The theory of swimming is not swimming. Philosophy is not reality. We only begin to experience the reality of swimming when we go into the water and start putting the theory into practice. Then we can gain a true knowledge of swimming. It is then that the theory becomes our reality.

In terms of theory and reality, sometimes people say of a truth or promise, "I know it in my head, but not in my heart." The heart is the place of spiritual experience and reality. So in this sense, what they are saying is: "I know the theory in my mind, but I am not experiencing the reality in my life. I have the concept, but not the experience."

Only the Spirit of God can take the theory of the word and establish it as a reality in our hearts and lives. He is the bridge between the intellectual knowledge of the head and the reality of the heart. He makes it real.

Word and Spirit

John 8:31-32

So Jesus was saying to those Jews who had believed Him, "If you continue in My word, then you are truly disciples of Mine; and you will know the truth, and the truth will make you free."

2 Corinthians 3:17 (NRSV)

Now the Lord is the Spirit, and where the Spirit of the Lord is, there is freedom.

John 8:36

"So if the Son makes you free, you will be free indeed."

If we abide in God's word, then we will know the truth and be set free. And if the Son makes us free, we will be free indeed: we will experience the reality of true spiritual freedom. In these passages, the word, the Spirit and Jesus are all connected in bringing us into freedom. The word reveals the truth of freedom and the Spirit leads us to experience the freedom that is found in Jesus.

In this way, if we want to live in reality then we need to abound in both the word and the Spirit of Jesus. To separate the Spirit and the word, or value one over the other, is to undermine the purpose of both. We need to richly combine the Spirit and the word in us to experience the depths of Jesus.

Summary

John 1:3

In the beginning was the Word, and the Word was with God, and the Word was God. He was in the beginning with God. All things came into being through Him, and apart from Him nothing came into being that has come into being.[7]

Jesus is the ultimate truth and reality. Everything that is real flows from the reality of Jesus. He is life and gives life. Jesus is the source and sustainer of reality.

Every aspect of our spiritual growth and life is found in Christ. All the spiritual realities that we can experience in God such as love, joy, peace, vision, passion, and so on, are simply aspects of the nature of Jesus. Thus to grow spiritually is to grow into Jesus. To live is Christ.[8]

To experience Jesus in these ways and live in His reality we need to unite the Spirit and the word within us. The word reveals the truth and the Spirit leads us into truth. So as we abide in God's word and Spirit, we will experience more of Jesus in our lives. By His grace, we will live in reality of God.

Questions

What are some of the spiritual realities that I have already experienced in some way?

What do I know in my head, but not in my heart?

What are some qualities of God that I want to experience?

Study 3

February 10, 2014

Worship in Truth

...for we are the true circumcision, who worship in the Spirit of God and glory in Christ Jesus...

Philippians 3:3

The word and the Spirit work together to lead us into truth. The word provides the theory and the Spirit leads us into the reality. To explore the difference between having theory and experiencing reality, we will look at what it is to worship in spirit and truth.

Spirit and Truth

John 4:23-24

"But an hour is coming, and now is, when the true worshipers will worship the Father in spirit and truth; for such people the Father seeks to be His worshipers. God is spirit, and those who worship Him must worship in spirit and truth."

17

God is spirit and so it is in the spirit that we encounter and worship God. As we learned in the *Spirit and Reality* study, the spirit of a person is symbolized by the heart.[1] Our heart is the center of our being. It is the power and substance of who we are and the place of our spiritual experience. Thus to worship God in spirit is to worship Him from the heart.

In the *Truth and Reality* study, we learned that truth is reality. In this sense, our call to worship God in truth is a call to worship Him in reality, with our worship being a genuine expression of our hearts. Too often we can worship God out of our minds, based on what we know of Him from the word. When we do this, we worship God intellectually rather than spiritually. This kind of worship is an adoration of our concept of Jesus rather than Jesus Himself. True worship is a spiritual act sourced in the spirit, not the intellect.

To move beyond the mind into worship of the heart, we need to discover the truth of worship in Scripture. We then need to seek God to lead us into the reality of true worship.

What is Worship?

Worship: *proskuneo*
To kiss the hand to (towards) one, in token of reverence; an expression of profound reverence, kneeling or prostration to do homage (to one) or make obeisance, whether in order to express respect or to make supplication.

The word *proskuneo* shows that worship involves profound reverence and obeisance. *Obeisance* means an act of homage or reverence, expressing a heart that is ready and willing to obey. Thus in worship we recognize the nature and love of God and we revere Him. We humble ourselves in surrender to God and we give ourselves to obeying His leading and calling. In worship we acknowledge that God is supreme and worthy of all love, devotion and obedience.

Ardent Love

Various dictionaries define worship in similar ways:
- Love unquestioningly and uncritically or to excess; to regard with deep or rapturous love; a feeling of profound love and admiration[2]
- To regard with ardent or adoring esteem or devotion[3]
- Extravagant respect or admiration for or devotion to an object of esteem[4]
- To show profound religious devotion and respect to; adore or venerate[5]

Worship in this sense is an expression of extravagant love and devotion. When we combine this with *proskuneo,* we find that worship is an expression of reverence, obedience, humility, devotion, and excessive, extravagant, rapturous love.

Thus true worship can only flow from a transformed heart. As such, if we are to worship in truth, we need to focus on our hearts. How can we possess such a surpassing love for God?

The Heart of Worship

Psalm 51:15-17

O Lord, open my lips,

That my mouth may declare Your praise.

For You do not delight in sacrifice, otherwise I
would give it;

You are not pleased with burnt offering.

The sacrifices of God are a broken spirit;

A broken and a contrite heart, O God, You will
not despise.

David recognized that God does not delight in outward acts of
sacrifice, but looks at the heart. So David asked God to open
his lips that he may declare God's praise. David needed the
Spirit of God to make his praise real and His worship a sincere
offering of the heart.

Like David, we also need God's grace to worship in truth.
We cannot create profound reverence, humility or awe by our
own efforts.[6] We are powerless to break our own spirit that we
may offer the sacrifice of a contrite heart. In short, without His
grace, we simply cannot worship God.

So if we truly want to experience real worship, we need
God to transform us. We need to seek God to release His love
for Jesus into us.[7] We need to ask the Spirit to reveal to us a
measure of God's awesome glory so that true reverence and
awe may rise within our hearts. And so our worship can flow
from a contrite heart, we need to cry out to God to humble us.
Then we need to prepare to be broken.

Matthew 21:44
"And he who falls on this stone will be broken to pieces; but on whomever it falls, it will scatter him like dust."

Being humbled and broken is a gift of God. When Jesus breaks us, He overcomes the elements within us that resist His grace. He conquers our independence, insecurity, religiousness and pride. In their place, He establishes His love and humility.

So if we want a heart that passionately loves Jesus, we can call out to God for His grace. We can fall on the rock of Christ and let Him break us. As we give ourselves to worship, He will create in us a humble and contrite heart. He will break our pride and prepare our hearts for His love.

John 17:26 (NKJV)
"And I have declared to them Your name, and will declare it, that the love with which You loved Me may be in them, and I in them."

Just as we cannot break our own hearts, so we cannot create real love by ourselves. Only God is love.[8] Only He can lead us to love Him with a deep and rapturous love. And He wants to. Here Jesus prays that the Father would fill us with His love for Jesus. It is a prayer that God wants to answer. If we are willing, God will give us His Spirit and fill our hearts with His love for Jesus. But are we willing? Do we really want to be humbled, broken and filled with love? Is this even possible?

Worship in Action

Luke 7:36-38

Now one of the Pharisees was requesting Him to dine with him, and He entered the Pharisee's house and reclined at the table. And there was a woman in the city who was a sinner; and when she learned that He was reclining at the table in the Pharisee's house, she brought an alabaster vial of perfume, and standing behind Him at His feet, weeping, she began to wet His feet with her tears, and kept wiping them with the hair of her head, and kissing His feet and anointing them with the perfume.[9]

Here we see true worship. It is pure adoration from a broken heart, poured out before God. It is an expression of devotion, humility and passionate love for Jesus. It is the fragrant aroma of a costly sacrifice; a precious, irretrievable offering made in blessing to Jesus.

Thus as this passage shows, by God's grace, true worship is possible. When our hearts are touched by Jesus, our worship will flow naturally through us. The love He pours into us will compel us to love and worship Him.

Worship is like a precious and beautiful perfume, creating a pleasing aroma to God. When we express our love in true worship, we minister to Jesus. Having received His love, we anoint Jesus with our love. Through worship, we return to God a measure of the blessing and love that He has given us.

Living Worship

Ephesians 5:1-2

Therefore be imitators of God, as beloved children, and live in love...[10]

Romans 12:1

Therefore I urge you, brethren, by the mercies of God, to present your bodies a living and holy sacrifice, acceptable to God, which is your spiritual service of worship.

We are called to worship God as a living sacrifice. Worship is more than an occasional act, song, or offering. It is more than words. Worship is a way of life.

So like the woman who anointed Jesus, we too can have times of deep, expressive worship. But worship does not end with the last drop of perfume. A heart that is devoted to Jesus continues in love. It is in this sense that we are called to be *living* sacrifices of worship. Our worship is to flow into our everyday lives. We are to carry the sense of love, humility, obedience and devotion to God into every part of our lives. We are to live in love.

Summary

In Scripture truth is reality. We are called to walk in the truth, by living in the reality of God.[11] This means as we discover the truth of the word, we need to seek the Spirit of God to fulfill the word in our lives. Only He can take the truth of the word from our heads and establish it in our hearts through personal experience. As the Spirit works in us, we enter into more of His truth and experience more of Jesus, and we are changed.

Thus in terms of worship, the word reveals the true nature of worship. As we respond with faith and desire, the Spirit of God begins to transform us. He reveals to us the awesome nature of God and creates reverence and awe in us. He breaks us and frees us from our pride and independence. He pours out His love into us and establishes the humility and love of Christ in our hearts.[12]

As the Spirit of God works in us, we start to change. As the love and revelation of Jesus grows, our worship naturally becomes more profound, genuine and sincere. In this way, we do not have to try to worship in spirit and truth. We simply need to seek God for His grace and love, so that we can truly worship Him. As we seek God, He takes us where we are and gently leads us into the reality of worship. By His grace, we are transformed more and more into true worshippers, true followers, and true lovers of Jesus.

Questions
What does it mean to be broken and transformed?
Do I want to be filled with love, even if it comes with tears?
What would a life of worship be like?

Study 4

February 17 2014

The Living Word

...for you have been born again not of seed
which is perishable but imperishable, that is, through
the living and enduring word of God.
1 Peter 1:23

Scripture is the written word of God. It is the record of the gospel—the revelation of God's love, forgiveness, power and life, made available to us through the death and resurrection of Jesus.

The word describes the nature of God and the life we can have in Him. As such, the written word of God provides the theoretical basis for life in Christ. But theory is not reality. Reality only comes as we enter into the personal experience of truth. To experience reality in our lives, we need the written word of God to become the living word.

The Living Word

Hebrews 4:12-13 (NRSV)
Indeed, the word of God is living and active, sharper than any two-edged sword, piercing until it divides soul from spirit, joints from marrow; it is able to judge the thoughts and intentions of the heart. And before him no creature is hidden, but all are naked and laid bare to the eyes of the one to whom we must render an account.

The word of God is not locked in the past, but is living and active. It can come to life and take effective action in us. So how do we experience the living and active word of God?

Word of Life

John 6:63
"It is the Spirit who gives life; the flesh profits nothing; the words that I have spoken to you are spirit and are life."

2 Corinthians 3:5-6
Not that we are adequate in ourselves to consider anything as coming from ourselves, but our adequacy is from God, who also made us adequate as servants of a new covenant, not of the letter but of the Spirit; for the letter kills, but the Spirit gives life.

All life flows from the Spirit. Our physical and spiritual life is sourced in and sustained by the Spirit of Jesus. The same is true of the word. The word of God only comes to life when the Spirit gives it life.

The Spirit of God also performs the word and brings it to pass in our lives. Thus the Spirit is the living and active power of the word. As such, to experience the living word we need to unite the Spirit of God with the word of God. We need the Spirit to breathe life into His word and fulfill that word in us.

The life that the Spirit breathes into the word is the life of Jesus. So when we receive the living word, we receive the life of Christ. Through the living word, the presence of Jesus is released into us and we are connected more with Him.

Life in the Word

Our spiritual growth in God begins with faith and desire. Once we believe the word can come alive, we need to desire it. We can then follow our desire and ask the Spirit of Jesus to bring His word to life for us. And He will, because He wants to. It is His desire is to lead us to know the reality of His living and active word.

Luke 24:32

They said to one another, "Were not our hearts burning within us while He was speaking to us on the road, while He was explaining the Scriptures to us?"

When the Spirit breathes on the word, we will find a sense of life in the Scripture and this can be a uniquely individual experience. Sometimes or for some people it may be like a burning within the heart. For others, the living word may bring a feeling of excitement or anticipation; a quickening that occurs on reading a certain passage of Scripture. At other times it may come as a quiet peace or a sense of the presence of God. Sometimes the Spirit may move in the word to bring a fresh renewal or release. Regardless of how the Spirit brings life in the word, there will always be an underlying sense of love, life and freedom. The living word will always be edifying, drawing us deeper into God.

In whatever way the Spirit brings the word to life for us, we can be sure that the life we sense in God's word is more than a simple emotion or feeling; it is a spiritual connection with the Spirit of God. It is the personal experience of the word coming to life for us.

Deeper into Jesus

So why does the Spirit bring the word to life? The Spirit of God brings His word to life because He wants to fulfill that word in us. The living word reveals the will of God for us. So when we encounter the living word, we can be sure that the grace of God is present to make it a reality in us.

For example, at times the Spirit may bring life to Scriptures that expose sin within us. As we receive His word, we can enter into the reality of forgiveness and freedom from that sin.

At other times, Scriptures about wisdom may come to life for us. As we take hold of the living word, we can experience the power of the Spirit to create more of His wisdom in us.

In this way, the Spirit brings the word to life to help us grow in God. Through the living word, we discover what God is doing in us at this time.

Our Natural Face

Thus the living word reveals the heart and will of God to us. His heart for us is one of surpassing love. His will is that we become who He created us to be. In this way, the living word lets us grow closer to God and shows us the truth of who we can become in Jesus.

> **James 1:22-25** (emphasis added)
> But prove yourselves doers of the word, and not merely hearers who delude themselves. For if anyone is a hearer of the word and not a doer, **he is like a man who looks at his natural face in a mirror**; for once he has looked at himself and gone away, he has immediately forgotten what kind of person he was. But one who looks intently at the perfect law, the law of liberty, and abides by it, not having become a forgetful hearer but an effectual doer, this man will be blessed in what he does.

Natural: *genesis*

Source, origin; used of birth, nativity; that which follows origin , viz. existence, life.

The word of God is like a mirror. When we look at Scripture we can see our natural face. Our natural face is who God created us to be. It is His original design for us; the image of who we truly are in Christ.

Thus through the word we see our potential in God: a life of holiness, godliness, love, joy, peace and wholeness. Yet simply having the promise of who we can be in God is not the same as living the reality. So if the Spirit brings the word to life then we need to take hold of the word and seek Him to fulfill it in us. For if we fail to act on what we see in the word, we can miss out on the personal experience of the word and forget what kind of people we truly are in God. As such we need to focus on the word, abide in it, and become doers of the living word, allowing God to bring His word to pass in our lives.

2 Corinthians 3:17-18

Now the Lord is the Spirit, and where the Spirit of the Lord is, there is liberty. But we all, with unveiled face, beholding as in a mirror the glory of the Lord, are being transformed into the same image from glory to glory, just as from the Lord, the Spirit.

But we, beholding His glory through the word of God, are being transformed into His image. The living word is the transforming word. Through the word, the Spirit fills us with the life and presence of Christ, and we are changed. His life transforms us from within. We are united with Jesus and we become more like Him.

Summary

As we grow in Christ we can experience the living and active word of God. The word of God comes to life when the Spirit breathes His life into it. In this way, the Spirit of Jesus is the life and action of the word; He makes His word alive and He brings it to pass in our lives. As such, we need to combine the word with the Spirit to experience the power of the living and active word of God.

The living word is a personal encounter of God that carries the life and presence of Jesus. So as we receive His living word, the Spirit imparts more of Jesus into us, transforming us into who we truly are in God: people who are created in His image, designed to live in love and unity with Him.

Questions

When has the Spirit brought the word to life for me? What was that like?

Do I want to experience more of the living word?

How can I unite the word and the Spirit in my life?

Study 5

February 24, 2014 (handwritten)

The Spoken Word

"It is written, 'Man shall not live on bread alone,
but on every word that proceeds out of the mouth of God.'"

Matthew 4:4

The Voice of God

John 10:1-5

"Truly, truly, I say to you, he who does not enter by the door into the fold of the sheep, but climbs up some other way, he is a thief and a robber. But he who enters by the door is a shepherd of the sheep. To him the doorkeeper opens, and the sheep hear his voice, and he calls his own sheep by name and leads them out. When he puts forth all his own, he goes ahead of them, and the sheep follow him because they know his voice. A stranger they simply will not follow, but will flee from him, because they do not know the voice of strangers."

Those who follow Jesus will know His voice. It is a promise of God that we will hear His voice if we believe. In order to hear Jesus' voice we need to have a living and real relationship with His Spirit. Our life in Christ is not to be built merely on theology and religion, but on a two-way relationship with God in which we speak with Him and He speaks with us.

The Spirit of Jesus can speak to us in many different ways, but for the purposes of this study we will focus on hearing Him speak through the written word of God. In *Series Three* we will look at hearing God in other ways.

Every Rhema

Matthew 4:1-4

Then Jesus was led up by the Spirit into the wilderness to be tempted by the devil. And after He had fasted forty days and forty nights, He then became hungry. And the tempter came and said to Him, "If You are the Son of God, command that these stones become bread." But He answered and said, "It is written, 'Man shall not live on bread alone, but on every word that proceeds out of the mouth of God.'"

We shall not live on bread alone, but on every word (*rhema*) that proceeds out of the mouth of God. In this passage we find that real life does not come from having enough food to survive. True spiritual life comes from God as we receive every *rhema* that comes from His mouth.

Word: *rhema*

That which is or has been uttered by the living voice, thing spoken, word.

The Greek word *rhema* means *a spoken word from a living voice.* The rhema word of God is the sound of His voice speaking to us. God is not silent, but active and vocal, longing to speak into our lives. If we let Him, He will speak directly to us. Then, as we hear Him speak, we will live on more than bread alone; we will find life in every word that comes from the mouth of God.

When we combine the word and Spirit, we find new life as God speaks to us through His word. When this happens the written word becomes the living word. The words we read are more than just words; they are the living voice of God.

Learning to Hear

John 10:27
"My sheep hear My voice, and I know them, and they follow Me."

Psalm 95:7
For He is our God, and we are the people of His pasture and the sheep of His hand. Today, if you would hear His voice...

Jesus wants to be our Shepherd and teach us how to hear His voice. To know Jesus' voice we firstly need to believe that He speaks. Really believe. Then we need to learn to hear Him.

> **John 16:13**
> "But when He, the Spirit of truth, comes, He will guide you into all the truth; for He will not speak on His own initiative, but whatever He hears, He will speak; and He will disclose to you what is to come."

God has given us His Spirit to speak to us and lead us into truth and reality.[1] So if we want to know the reality of hearing God, then we start by asking the Spirit to open our ears and teach us how to listen to Him.

In learning to hear God, it can be helpful to remember that the Spirit of Jesus is on our side. He wants to help us to hear Him clearly. So if we feel that we are unable to hear God then it is a problem for the Spirit. And He will solve it. Our part is to eagerly desire to know His voice. His part is to teach us, speak to us, and lead us into the reality of hearing His voice.

Once we believe that God speaks, we need to continually yield any doubt to God and maintain a heart of faith and desire. As we open the Scriptures, we need to give our time to God and let Him lead us. Then, when the Spirit breathes life into a particular verse or passage, it will ignite something in our spirit. Our spirit will witness with Him and we will know that God is speaking directly to us through His living word.

For example, as God forms His humility in us, He may speak to us through Scriptures that focus on humility such as Colossians 3:12-13. As He takes us deeper into His peace, He may breathe life into passages like Philippians 4:7. When God speaks to us through His living word, we can be sure that the power of the Spirit is present to take us into the reality. But how do we know that we are really hearing God's voice?

2 Corinthians 13:1
This is the third time I am coming to you. Every fact [*rhema*] is to be confirmed by the testimony of two or three witnesses.

Every *rhema* is confirmed by two or three witnesses. So when God speaks to us, He will confirm His voice at least two or three times. These confirmations can come in a number of different ways, just as we can hear God's voice in various ways.[2] When God confirms His word, we can have complete confidence in what He has said. We can be sure that the Spirit will fulfill the word He has spoken and lead us into the reality. What He says goes. His word will never fail.

Summary
It is a promise of God that we will hear His voice. Hearing God speak is not a privilege reserved for mature believers, but a promise made to everyone who follows Jesus. We can all hear Jesus speak personally to us.

One of the many ways that God speaks to us is through His written word. As His word comes to life we can hear Him speak directly to us. By speaking into our lives, the Spirit of God releases the creative power of God into us. So if the Spirit wants to impart the zeal of Christ into us, He may lead us to Scriptures that speak of His passion and zeal. When we read these Scriptures, we find a sense of life in them and know that this is God's desire for us at this time. We can have complete confidence that God is leading us into the reality of His zeal because He has spoken. And when He speaks, things happen.

Thus hearing God's voice is a key to growing in Christ. If we genuinely seek God to teach us to hear Him with clarity, He will fulfill His promise to us. We will hear His voice and know the power of His spoken word in us.

Questions
Can I hear God?

Do I want to hear God more?

In what ways have I heard God speak?

Study 6 *march 3, 2014*

Ω

Word of Power

Then God said, "Let there be light"; and there was light.

Genesis 1:3

God Speaks and it is Done

Psalm 33:6-9

By the word of the LORD the heavens were made,

And by the breath of His mouth all their host.

He gathers the waters of the sea together as a

heap,

He lays up the deeps in storehouses.

Let all the earth fear the LORD;

Let all the inhabitants of the world stand in awe

of Him.

For He spoke, and it was done;

He commanded, and it stood fast.

God spoke and it was done. He commanded and it stood fast. The Scriptures are clear: when God says something, it is done. When He spoke forth light, there was light.[1] When He spoke forth healing, there was healing.[2] So to grow in Christ, we simply need to invite God to speak into our lives. Then, as the Spirit speaks forth love, there will be love in us. If He speaks of healing, we will experience healing. When God speaks, His word will be done in our lives.

> **Isaiah 14:24-27** (NKJV)
> The LORD of hosts has sworn, saying, "Surely, as I have thought, so it shall come to pass, and as I have purposed, so it shall stand: That I will break the Assyrian in My land, and on My mountains tread him underfoot. Then his yoke shall be removed from them, and his burden removed from their shoulders. This is the purpose that is purposed against the whole earth, and this is the hand that is stretched out over all the nations. For the LORD of hosts has purposed, and who will annul it? His hand is stretched out, and who will turn it back?"

As I have thought, so it shall come to pass, and as I have purposed, so it shall stand.

God is awesome in power. As He thinks, so it comes to pass; as He purposes, so it happens. God simply has to think something for it to happen. So if the thoughts and plans of

God come to pass, how much more will His living words be fulfilled in our lives? Every word that He speaks to us will come to pass, for nothing can defeat Him or His promises. God keeps His word.

The Word Works

Isaiah 55:8-11

"For My thoughts are not your thoughts, nor are your ways My ways," declares the LORD. "For as the heavens are higher than the earth, so are My ways higher than your ways and My thoughts than your thoughts. For as the rain and the snow come down from heaven, and do not return there without watering the earth and making it bear and sprout, and furnishing seed to the sower and bread to the eater; so will My word be which goes forth from My mouth; it will not return to Me empty, without accomplishing what I desire, and without succeeding in the matter for which I sent it."

1 Thessalonians 2:13

For this reason we also constantly thank God that when you received the word of God which you heard from us, you accepted it not as the word of men, but for what it really is, the word of God, which also performs its work in you who believe.

The word of God performs its work in those who believe. The word which God speaks to us will always accomplish its purpose and fulfill its goal. So what is the work of the word of God?

The work of the word of God's peace is to draw us into the reality of His peace. The word of His joy is given that we might experience His joy. The same is true for every word that God speaks, whether it is the word of His love, holiness, forgiveness, boldness or life. He speaks forth His word to lead us into the reality of what He has spoken.

Words of Life

John 6:60-63

Therefore many of His disciples, when they heard this said, "This is a difficult statement; who can listen to it?" But Jesus, conscious that His disciples grumbled at this, said to them, "Does this cause you to stumble? What then if you see the Son of Man ascending to where He was before? It is the Spirit who gives life; the flesh profits nothing; the words that I have spoken to you are spirit and are life."

The words that Jesus spoke were spirit and life. The Holy Spirit infused Jesus' words, so that what He said carried the life and creative power of the Spirit. Whoever received His words received the spiritual power of God.

In the same way, if we receive and believe the word that God speaks to us, we will know the power of God to fulfill His word in us. His word will no longer be a theory but a reality in our lives. We will experience the reality not because we know a secret method or formula, but simply because God is true to His word. Through the Spirit, God will fulfill His word in us.

Power in the Word

John 15:1-3

"I am the true vine, and My Father is the vinedresser. Every branch in Me that does not bear fruit, He takes away; and every branch that bears fruit, He prunes it so that it may bear more fruit. You are already clean because of the word which I have spoken to you."

Ephesians 5:25-27

Husbands, love your wives, just as Christ also loved the church and gave Himself up for her, so that He might sanctify her, having cleansed her by the washing of water with the word, that He might present to Himself the church in all her glory, having no spot or wrinkle or any such thing; but that she would be holy and blameless.

The power of the word can be seen in these passages. The disciples were clean because of the word Jesus spoke to them.

Like the disciples, as we receive the word of God's forgiveness and cleansing, we will be cleansed by the washing of water by the word.[3] The word will do its work in us.

In this way, the more we abide in the living word of God, the more we can grow in Christ and live in reality. We simply need to hear God speak, give ourselves to His will, and let the Spirit fulfill His word in us.

Summary

Numbers 23:19
God is not a man, that He should lie, nor a son of man, that He should repent; has He said, and will He not do it? Or has He spoken, and will He not make it good?

God's word is sure, for as Scripture says: strong is He who carries out His word.[4] God is not a man that He should lie, but what He says He will do, and what He has spoken He will make good. When God speaks a word into our lives, He watches over it to make sure that it comes to pass, so we can be certain that none of the promises that God gives us will ever fail.[5] The word that God speaks to us can be trusted. If we put our confidence in Him we will not be disappointed.[6] By His Spirit, God will keep His word and lead us to experience the reality of what He has spoken.

Questions

What can stop God from performing His word?

What part do we play in seeing His word brought to pass?

Has He spoken something that is yet to be fulfilled in me?

Study 7 *march 10, 2014*

Ω

Our Inheritance

In Him also we have obtained an inheritance...
to the end that we who were the first to hope in Christ
would be to the praise of His glory.
Ephesians 1:11

Heirs of God

Romans 8:16-17a
The Spirit Himself testifies with our spirit that we are children of God, and if children, heirs also, heirs of God and fellow heirs with Christ...

When we become children of God, the Father makes us heirs of a spiritual inheritance. This inheritance is our potential life in Christ and all the blessings we can have as we grow in Him. But how can we discover and experience the riches of our inheritance? What is our inheritance in God?

An Eternal Inheritance

Hebrews 9:15-17

For this reason He is the mediator of a new covenant, so that, since a death has taken place for the redemption of the transgressions that were committed under the first covenant, those who have been called may receive the promise of the eternal inheritance. For where a covenant is, there must of necessity be the death of the one who made it. For a covenant is valid only when men are dead, for it is never in force while the one who made it lives.

Covenant: *diatheke*

A disposition, arrangement, of any sort, which one wishes to be valid, the last disposition which one makes of his earthly possessions after his death, a testament or will.

Jesus is the mediator of the new covenant. This covenant is like a last will and testament. In the natural realm when a person dies, they leave what they own as an inheritance to others, usually their family. The same is true of God. When Jesus died, God gave His children everything that was His. Thus the death of Jesus did not just secure our redemption and forgiveness—it gave us an inheritance. Through Christ's death we have inherited a life-changing spiritual estate. It has been given to us, it is ours, and nothing can take it away.

Beyond Imagination

1 Corinthians 2:9
Things which eye has not seen and ear has not heard, and which have not entered the heart of man, all that God has prepared for those who love Him.

No mind can conceive what God has prepared for those who love Him. When we set our love on God, He sets before us an inheritance that is beyond our imagination. He call us to a life of spiritual wealth that exceeds our greatest hopes or dreams. But how do we experience that wealth? How can we know the reality of our inheritance if it is beyond our comprehension?

Ephesians 1:18-19a
I pray that the eyes of your heart may be enlightened, so that you may know what is the hope of His calling, what are the riches of the glory of His inheritance in the saints, and what is the surpassing greatness of His power toward us who believe.

May the eyes of our hearts be enlightened that we may know the riches of our inheritance in God. To truly understand the nature of our calling and inheritance, we need God to open the eyes of our hearts. Apart from God, we will never be able to comprehend what He has given us. Only He can reveal to us the glory and wonder of the life He has prepared for us.

Christ our Inheritance

Psalm 16:1-6

Preserve me, O God, for I take refuge in You. I said to the LORD, "You are my Lord; I have no good besides You." As for the saints who are in the earth, they are the majestic ones in whom is all my delight. The sorrows of those who have bartered for another god will be multiplied; I shall not pour out their drink offerings of blood, nor will I take their names upon my lips. The LORD is the portion of my inheritance and my cup; You support my lot. The lines have fallen to me in pleasant places; indeed, my heritage is beautiful to me.

In this passage we see that the Lord is the portion of our inheritance. Jesus is our inheritance. As such, our inheritance *in* Christ is really our inheritance *of* Christ. It is not just the blessings we can experience in God. Our inheritance is Jesus. It is the gift of His life, nature and presence within us. Jesus is the awesome gift of God.

Galatians 5:22-23

But the fruit of the Spirit is love, joy, peace, patience, kindness, goodness, faithfulness, gentleness, self-control; against such things there is no law.

1 Corinthians 1:30-31
But by His doing you are in Christ Jesus, who
became to us wisdom from God, and
righteousness and sanctification, and redemption,
so that, just as it is written, "let him who boasts,
boast in the LORD."

Our inheritance in righteousness, sanctification, wisdom and
redemption is our inheritance in Jesus, for He is all these
things. In the same way, our inheritance of love is the gift of
Jesus, who is Love.[1] Our inheritance of joy is found in the
presence of Christ, who is Joy.[2] All the fruits of the Spirit and
the different aspects of our inheritance are qualities that flow
from the nature and life of Jesus. He is our inheritance and the
source of our every blessing.

Colossians 1:26-27
That is the mystery which has been hidden from
the past ages and generations, but has now been
manifested to His saints, to whom God willed to
make known what is the riches of the glory of
this mystery among the Gentiles, which is Christ
in you, the hope of glory.

The mystery of the gospel is *Christ in us*. The life of Jesus is the
unimaginable gift that God has prepared for us. By His grace,
we can become one spirit with Christ and live our life in unity
with Him.[3] This is a profound mystery but an absolute reality.

We can live in Christ and He in us. He can become our every heartbeat and breath. He can become our life, love and glory. Jesus is our inheritance and this is our calling.

But will we give ourselves to our high calling? Is all of this even possible? Can Jesus really live in us?

Unto Him

Ephesians 3:20-21

Now to Him who is able to do far more abundantly beyond all that we ask or think, according to the power that works within us, to Him be the glory in the church and in Christ Jesus to all generations forever and ever. Amen.

Life beyond our comprehension is before us. God is awesome in power and love, and He is able to do abundantly more than we could ever imagine. For as the Amplified version reads: God is able to do "superabundantly, far over and above all that we dare ask or think, infinitely beyond our highest prayers, desires, thoughts, hopes, or dreams." According to the power of His Spirit within us, Jesus can exceed our highest expectations, our deepest hopes and our greatest dreams. But does He really want to? Yes, He really wants to.

So why not dream a little? Can we dream of being united with Jesus in love? God can do it and He wants to. Can we imagine life immersed in God's presence, such that His love radiates out of every part of us? God can do that and more.

Can we imagine the power of the Spirit flowing through us, devastating the darkness and changing the world around us? God can surpass even that. Can we imagine loving God with every part of our being? God can make it a reality for us. He is unlimited in His power and love and He can do far more than we can possibly imagine. So let us dream of the abundant life that God has called us to, knowing that He has the power and desire to make it a reality. He can do it.

Summary

Through the death of Jesus, God has given us an awesome spiritual inheritance. Our inheritance is not only the blessings of relationship that we can have with God or the various fruit of the Spirit, but it is Christ Himself. Jesus is our inheritance. His life is more than we could imagine or hope for, but it is this life we are called to. And it can be done.

In His power, the Spirit of God can lead us to possess our inheritance in Christ. We can live in Jesus and He in us. We can become one with Christ. Jesus longs to take us into the reality of our inheritance in Him. He is ready and waiting. All we need to do is share His desire, believe in Him, and let the adventure begin.

Questions

Have I set my love on God?

What has God prepared for me?

What could my life in unity with Christ be like?

Study 8 *man 17, 2014*

Ɋ

Inheritance of Life

And now I commend you to God and to the word of His grace,
which is able to build you up and to give you the inheritance
among all those who are sanctified.

Acts 20:32

The word of God's grace is able to give us an inheritance among those who are sanctified. The inheritance that we have been given is Jesus. It is the gift of His life, nature, love and presence, and all the qualities that are found in Him. But how do we receive the gift of Christ?

Divine Power

2 Peter 1:2-4

Grace and peace be multiplied to you in the knowledge of God and of Jesus our Lord; seeing that His divine power has granted to us everything pertaining to life and godliness, through the true knowledge of Him who called us by His own glory and excellence. For by these He has granted to us His precious and magnificent promises, so that by them you may become partakers of the divine nature, having escaped the corruption that is in the world by lust.

God has given us precious promises of our inheritance in Jesus. He has promised us His love, life, holiness, godliness, humility, gentleness, strength, peace, joy and grace. All these promises are found in the nature of Christ. And so God calls us to partake of His nature. He wants us to take the nature of Jesus into us and have the different aspects of His character formed in our hearts. He wants to live in us and lead us to live in the radiance of His nature and life.

Thus God has not called us to live an impossible life. Our inheritance in Christ is not a fantasy or a dream. God is good and in His grace He has given us everything we need for life and godliness. And that everything is Jesus.

1 Thessalonians 5:23-24
Now may the God of peace Himself sanctify you entirely; and may your spirit and soul and body be preserved complete, without blame at the coming of our Lord Jesus Christ. Faithful is He who calls you, and He also will bring it to pass.

As we partake of Jesus, His presence, nature and life are established in us and we begin to live in unity with Him. This can be our reality, not because we can do it, but because Jesus can do it. He has the power and desire to transform us into our high calling. So if we yield to His desire, He will lead us into the reality of our calling, for as Scripture says: faithful is He who calls us, He also will bring it to pass.

Inheriting Our Life

Colossians 3:9-10

Do not lie to one another, since you laid aside the old self with its evil practices, and have put on the new self who is being renewed to a true knowledge according to the image of the One who created him...

Our inheritance includes the promise of who we can become in Christ. So as we enter our inheritance in Jesus, we enter into our new self. This new self is who we were always designed to be: people who are created in the image of God to live in wholeness, love and unity with Christ.

Our transformation into the new self involves a change of our inward nature as it is united with the nature of Christ. For example, when we enter into our inheritance of love, we receive and experience His love. Then as we let His love infuse our hearts, it brings about our transformation. His love redefines us and recreates us more in the likeness of Love. The same is true for all the dimensions of Christ. As we experience

Jesus, He changes us and we become inherently different. We are not who we were. His nature overwhelms our nature and we are conformed more to His likeness.

The Greatest Command

Our inheritance of new life in Christ is expressed in many ways in Scripture. One such way is through commands. We are called to love each other fervently from the heart, because fervent love is a part of our inheritance.[1] We are commanded to forgive each other because we have an inheritance in the nature of Christ and it is in His nature to forgive.

In this way, every command of God can be regarded as a promise of our inheritance.[2] But is it really true? Can we live a pure, faithful, loving and righteous life? Is it possible to live in obedience to the commands and calls of God in Scripture?

To find out, we can start with the greatest command. For if the greatest command can be attained and kept then it stands to reason that every command and call in Scripture is attainable.[3]

> **Matthew 22:35-38**
> One of them, a lawyer, asked Him [Jesus] a question, testing Him, "Teacher, which is the great commandment in the Law?" And He said to him, "'You shall love the LORD your God with all your heart, and with all your soul, and with all your mind.' This is the great and foremost commandment."

Jesus says that to love God with all our heart, soul and mind is the greatest and most important command. This means that all the other commands and calls in Scripture can be viewed as an outworking of our complete love for God.

Therefore, if we can live in the reality of the greatest command and love God with everything we are, then every aspect of our inheritance is attainable. So is it actually possible to completely love God? Is this command really a promise of our inheritance in Christ?

> **Deuteronomy 30:6, 11**
> "Moreover the LORD your God will circumcise your heart and the heart of your descendants, to love the LORD your God with all your heart and with all your soul, so that you may live...For this commandment which I command you today is not too difficult for you, nor is it out of reach."

These verses confirm that the greatest command in Scripture is *not too difficult for you, nor is it out of reach*. We can love God with all our heart and soul, not because we can do it, but because He can do it in us. God alone has the power of love and He wants to release it in us. He wants to circumcise our hearts so that by His grace and power we may love Him with all our heart and soul, and live in Him. His love makes our love possible.

Given to Love

The greatest command is our highest call and yet it can only be fulfilled by God. He is the only One who can enable us to love Him with all our hearts. So how could we be judged for failing to love Him completely if Jesus is the only one that can make it a reality?

Our call to love God with all our heart, soul, mind and strength, is not a command to do it alone. It is a call to believe it is possible, to truly desire it, and then to seek God to lead us into the reality. So if we resolve to enter our inheritance of loving God with everything we are, if we devote ourselves to keeping the greatest command at any cost, then we need not fear any judgment upon failure for our part is done. We have given ourselves to loving God, we believe it is possible and we passionately desire it. The rest is the work of God. If we have faith and are willing, the Spirit will do His work in us. He will circumcise our hearts that we may love God with all our heart, soul, mind and strength.

Summary

Our inheritance in Christ is one of life. As we enter into our inheritance and partake of Jesus, we experience a fusion of His nature with our nature. He lives within us and we start to become one with Christ. As we are united with Jesus, we enter more into our new self, which is created in the image of God. Our new self is who God designed us to be. Thus to enter into our inheritance in Christ is to possess His life within us and experience our true life in union with Him.

We are called to live in the reality of the greatest command and love God with all our heart, soul and mind. This is not an impossible call or noble ideal, for God has given us everything we need for this life and godliness. He has promised that He will circumcise our hearts and fill us with the nature and life of Christ that we may love Him with all our heart. His power, grace and love have made it all possible. Our part is simply to devote our lives to loving Him completely and let Him do the rest.

As the nature of Christ is formed in us, we will realize that Scripture is true and that with God nothing is too difficult nor out of reach. Nothing. We can be pure as He is pure and holy as He is holy, because Jesus is pure and holy and He lives within us. He is our inheritance and He is our life.

Questions

Is it possible to love God with all my heart?

How can I truly believe it?

Will I devote my life to loving God with everything I am?

Study 9 *march 24, 2014*

Inheritance and Possession

*So the LORD gave Israel all the land which He had sworn to give
to their fathers, and they possessed it and lived in it.*
Joshua 21:43

Ownership and Possession

Psalm 105:44

He gave them also the lands of the nations, that
they might take possession of the fruit of the
peoples' labor.

God has given us an inheritance that we might take
possession of it. For something to be our inheritance means
that we have a legal entitlement to it. However, for something
to be our possession means that we personally experience and
live in the reality of it. Inheritance is the theory; possession is
the reality—our actual experience.

In the natural realm we may inherit great riches, but if we fail to take possession of our inheritance and let it change our lives, then it is of no value. The same is true spiritually. We have an inheritance that surpasses all imagination, but for it to be of any value we need to experience it and be transformed by it. Only as we venture out and take possession of our inheritance does it become a defining reality in our lives.

The Lonely King

This relationship between inheritance and possession can be illustrated in a short story.

—

A great but lonely king once decided that he would adopt a child. So he ordered a search of his kingdom for someone who would be as a son or daughter to him. After a time, a willing child was found: a poor street-boy who was found stealing and scrounging for food. The king was ecstatic. He went to meet his new son, embraced him and said, "My son, I love you. Though you are yet to know me, I am now your father. I am yours and you are mine. You are my heir. Everything I have I give to you. My love, my life and the entire kingdom are now your inheritance."

The street-boy was overjoyed. He thanked his new father, and then went back to tell all his street-friends. He told them everything that happened and of the riches that were now his. He also spoke of how his new father wanted to adopt everyone into his family. Many others responded and became sons and daughters of the king. They too began to tell others of the gift of their adoption and inheritance in the kingdom. And so the news spread. For many days the street-boy stayed with his street friends, full of excitement over the discovery of his new life. However, soon the days became weeks and the weeks became months.

The king remained in his palace longing for his son who was still living in the streets, zealously telling people of the good news of his inheritance. Occasionally the king would visit his son on the streets of the city to remind him of the riches that were his and to invite him home. Yet while the king longed for the presence and love of a child, the regal street-boy stayed on the streets of his old life, content in the knowledge of what the king had given him. The love and intimacy the king had sought was not found, and he remained the great but lonely king.

—

So having become children of God, where will we live? Will we be satisfied with the theory of our inheritance or pursue the reality? Will we live in the love that God so desires?

The Prodigal

The concept of inheritance and possession is illustrated in the parable of the prodigal son. In this parable, after the wayward son returned home into the arms and blessing of the father, the older brother became angry and resentful.

Luke 15:28-31

"But he became angry and was not willing to go in; and his father came out and began pleading with him. But he answered and said to his father, 'Look! For so many years I have been serving you and I have never neglected a command of yours; and yet you have never given me a young goat, so that I might celebrate with my friends; but when this son of yours came, who has devoured your wealth with prostitutes, you killed the fattened calf for him.' And he said to him, 'Son, you have always been with me, and all that is mine is yours...'"

The older brother was angry and jealous of the younger because even though He was living with the father, he was not living in the reality of his inheritance. He was rich and yet poor. Everything that belonged to the father was his; however it was his only in theory and not in experience. The older brother failed to ask for and enter into the blessings and riches of his inheritance. Furthermore, he failed to share those blessings with his friends. And now he resented seeing his brother enjoy the blessings he could have had all along. The message here is clear: we cannot afford to settle for the theory of our inheritance without the experience. As such, we need to continually seek to live more in the reality of our inheritance in Christ.

Relationship

The principle of ownership and possession is also true for the different relationships we have with God. When we first come to faith in Jesus we begin to know Him as our Redeemer. He is the one who redeems us from our bondage to sin and restores us into relationship with God. However, beyond redemption, the different relationships we can have with God are all a part of our spiritual inheritance. As we grow in God, we can begin to know and experience Him as our Savior, Father, Mother, Brother, Teacher, Provider, Protector, Counselor, Shepherd, Judge, Master, Friend, Helper, Lord, Bridegroom, Husband, and God, to name a few.[1] Each of these relationships lets us experience God in different ways and grow in Him.

For example, as we yield to God and learn to obey Him we discover Jesus as Lord. As we learn to listen to the Spirit and walk with Him, we come to relate to Jesus as our helper.[2] Likewise, as we read His word and learn and grow in God, we begin to know Jesus as our teacher and so on.

The only way to enter into these relationships is through experience. Therefore, until we know the reality of God as our judge, that dimension of relationship remains an unrealized part of our inheritance. God is love, but is He *my love*? Jesus is life, but is He *my life*? Is He my teacher, my master, my friend? All of these relationships are open to us, but we can only experience and possess them as the Spirit of God leads us into the reality of each relationship.

Fruitful Life

Matthew 21:42-46

Jesus said to them, "Did you never read in the Scriptures, 'the stone which the builders rejected, this became the chief corner stone; this came about from the LORD, and it is marvelous in our eyes'? Therefore I say to you, the kingdom of God will be taken away from you and given to a people, producing the fruit of it. And he who falls on this stone will be broken to pieces; but on whomever it falls, it will scatter him like dust." When the chief priests and the Pharisees heard His parables, they understood that He was speaking about them.

In Scripture, the chief priests and the Pharisees had the opportunity to receive a spiritual inheritance in Jesus. If they had repented and fallen on the rock of Jesus, they would have inherited the abundant life of Christ through faith and grace. However, the Pharisees preferred their religion to the living Christ and so they rejected their inheritance. They lacked the faith and desire for God. They were spiritually unfruitful and so missed out on the riches of the kingdom of Jesus.

Despite the many doctrines and teachings that they had of God, the Pharisees failed to recognize the Messiah when He came as their inheritance. Their religion had become a barrier to knowing God. Thus we need to learn from the Pharisees and maintain a heart that always seeks to know and love God.

We cannot let ourselves be satisfied with doctrines and theologies that do not lead to reality. Instead we need to hunger for the experience of our inheritance. We need to cry out to God for reality.

Summary

John 1:12

But as many as received Him, to them He gave the right to become children of God, even to those who believe in His name...

Having received Jesus, we have the right to become God's children and enter into our inheritance in Christ. Yet simply having the right to an inheritance does not mean that we experience the reality. We need to act on our right to take possession of what we have been given. We need to hunger for reality and call on God to lead us into our inheritance. And He will. He died to give us an inheritance and He will fulfill His promise to us. He will lead us ever deeper into the riches and glory of Jesus.

Questions

Where am I now spiritually?

What would my spiritual life be like if anything I desired of Christ was possible?

Is there anything preventing me from going deeper into my inheritance?

Study 10 *march 31, 2014*

Desire

"Blessed are those who hunger and thirst for righteousness,
for they shall be satisfied."
Matthew 5:6

If we hunger and thirst for Jesus, we will be satisfied. Our journey into our inheritance in Christ starts with faith and desire. Once we believe that God has prepared a life for us, we need to really hunger for it. We need to want to possess our inheritance and then actively pursue the reality.

Source of Desire

Philippians 2:13

...for it is God who is at work in you, both to will and to work for His good pleasure.

Will: *thelo*

To will, have in mind, intend, to be resolved or determined, to purpose, to desire, to wish, to love, to like to do a thing, be fond of doing, to take delight in, have pleasure.

Real desire for Jesus and our inheritance in Him comes from God. God works in us to will (*thelo*) and work for His good pleasure. So as we open our hearts and seek Him, He will form in us the will, desire, love, delight, and resolve for Jesus. It is His work and He wants to do it.

Wanting Desire

But do we really want God to form a deep desire for Jesus in our hearts? Desire comes with desire. As such, even if we feel that we have no real desire for Jesus at all, we can start by wanting the desire. Do we want to want Him?

Matthew 20:29-33

As they were leaving Jericho, a large crowd followed Him. And two blind men sitting by the road, hearing that Jesus was passing by, cried out, "Lord, have mercy on us, Son of David!" The crowd sternly told them to be quiet, but they cried out all the more, "Lord, Son of David, have mercy on us!" And Jesus stopped and called them, and said, "What do you want Me to do for you?" They said to Him, "Lord, we want our eyes to be opened." Moved with compassion, Jesus touched their eyes; and immediately they regained their sight and followed Him.

So what is our heart's desire? What would we answer if Jesus asked us "what do you want Me to do for you?" A good place to start is to be honest with God about where we are now and our desire for Him. Where are we spiritually? Where do we want to be? What do we want Jesus to do for us?

Isaiah 42:3
"A bruised reed He will not break and a dimly burning wick He will not extinguish; He will faithfully bring forth justice."

We should not fear any judgment or shame over our level of desire for God. God knows how much or how little we want and love Him. As such, being honest with God is more for our own benefit than His. We can take heart that we are growing and changing, and that where we are heading in God is more important than where we are now.

Knowing this, we can feel free to present our desire to God and ask Him to increase it. If we have only a flickering flame of desire for God, then we start with that and flow naturally with the little desire we have. He longs for us to have an awesome love and zeal for Him so He will never snuff out our smoldering wick—He will nourish and grow our desire for Him until it turns into the passion He longs for.

Growing Desire

The desire that God wants to form in us is the real desire of the heart. This desire is more than an intellectual persuasion or casual whim. It is a powerful motivating force within us, focusing our resolve and compelling us toward its goal. When we seek God to create this kind of desire in our hearts, we then need to keep in step with the Spirit as He works in us.

> **Galatians 6:7-9**
> Do not be deceived, God is not mocked; for whatever a man sows, this he will also reap. For the one who sows to his own flesh will from the flesh reap corruption, but the one who sows to the Spirit will from the Spirit reap eternal life. Let us not lose heart in doing good, for in due time we will reap if we do not grow weary.

In our spiritual lives we will reap what we sow. If we sow seeds of love, we will reap more love. If we sow seeds of faith, we will reap a harvest of faith. In the same way, if we sow seeds of desire for Jesus, we will reap a greater spiritual desire within us.

Seeds are sown into our hearts in many ways including through words, thoughts, images, prayer, reading, reflecting, music, conversations, media and so on. If we want to work with the Spirit in creating desire for Jesus in us then we can increase the seeds of life that we sow in our hearts. This means we can spend more time in those activities that bring us life and draw us closer to Jesus. We can spend more time with people who impart life to us, more time reading and watching material that builds our desire for God, and more time with God. We do this not because we should do it, but because God is forming His desire in us and so we naturally want to do it.

In sowing into our hearts, it is important to be discerning and to remember the principle of life. If the Spirit of God is in an activity, there will be a sense of life, freedom and blessing in it. As such, we are under no obligation to partake of anything that has no life, be it religious or secular. So as we grow, we can take control what we watch, read, hear and do, and choose to only partake of those things that have a sense of life. If we find that we are sowing destructive seed out of habit then we need to seek God to change us and form new habits. As He works in us, we will begin to find the seed of life and reality more enjoyable and satisfying than any worldly seed.

Maintaining Desire

Revelation 3:17-18

"Because you say, 'I am rich, and have become wealthy, and have need of nothing,' and you do not know that you are wretched and miserable and poor and blind and naked, I advise you to buy from Me gold refined by fire so that you may become rich, and white garments so that you may clothe yourself, and that the shame of your nakedness will not be revealed; and eye salve to anoint your eyes so that you may see."

This passage highlights the need for us to maintain our desire for more of God. The church of Laodicea thought they were living in their inheritance, when in reality they were living in a fantasy. They thought they were rich and wealthy, but really they were poor, blind and naked. Because they believed they were already living in their inheritance, they had no desire or hunger for more of God. Their desire had died. So Jesus opened their eyes to their true state of spiritual poverty that they might hunger for Him. His desire was that they would turn to Him and know the reality of their spiritual inheritance. So He called them to repent, seek Him and receive the grace they needed to possess their inheritance in Christ.

In the same way, as we enter into our inheritance, we need to be careful not to settle for the measure of our experience thus far and let our desire for more fade. Our inheritance in Christ is always beyond our imagination. So while we may have experienced a degree of what is available, the fullness is always more than we can imagine. We can always go farther and deeper. Our only limit is our faith and desire.

Summary

Desire is a key aspect of growing in God. As we possess real desire, it compels us to pursue more our inheritance in Jesus. Because this kind of desire is of the heart rather than the mind, we cannot create real desire by our own efforts. It is a gift of God. To receive this desire, we simply need to open our hearts to God and ask Him to do His work in us.

As the Spirit creates desire within us, we can actively add to that desire by sowing seeds of life into our hearts. As our desire builds and we experience more of our inheritance, we can then continue to build even more desire, for we know that there are no limits to the depths of our spiritual inheritance. There is always more of God to explore and enjoy. In Christ we are able to know the love that surpasses knowledge and to be filled with the fullness of the living God.[1] He makes it possible and He wants to make it a reality in us. A life beyond comprehension awaits us. So do we want it?

Questions

What desire do I have for Jesus?

What do I want Jesus to do for me?

How can I open my heart for more desire?

Study 11

ApRic 7, 2014

Access by Faith

*...in Christ Jesus our Lord, in whom we have boldness
and confident access through faith in Him.*
Ephesians 3:11b-12

Through the death of Jesus, God has given us an awesome
inheritance. He has given us Jesus: the gift of His presence, life
and nature within us. However, for His gift to be of value in
our lives, we need to actually experience it. We need to take
hold of our inheritance and make it our possession.

Hebrews 11:8-10
By faith Abraham, when he was called, obeyed by
going out to a place which he was to receive for
an inheritance; and he went out, not knowing
where he was going. By faith he lived as an alien
in the land of promise, as in a foreign land,
dwelling in tents with Isaac and Jacob, fellow

heirs of the same promise; for he was looking for the city which has foundations, whose architect and builder is God.

Abraham was called to possess an inheritance without any idea of where it was or what it would be like. Like Abraham, God has prepared an inheritance for us that is beyond our understanding. And like Abraham, we have to trust God that our inheritance is worth it; worth our time, our obedience, and our sacrifice to possess. In faith, we need to begin our journey into a life whose architect and builder is God. So are we ready to leave our old life and take possession of our inheritance?

Taking Hold of the Reality

Philippians 3:8-14

More than that, I count all things to be loss in view of the surpassing value of knowing Christ Jesus my Lord, for whom I have suffered the loss of all things, and count them but rubbish so that I may gain Christ, and may be found in Him, not having a righteousness of my own derived from the Law, but that which is through faith in Christ, the righteousness which comes from God on the basis of faith, that I may know Him and the power of His resurrection and the fellowship of His sufferings, being conformed to His death; in order that I may attain to the resurrection from the dead.

> Not that I have already obtained it or have already become perfect, but I press on so that I may lay hold of that for which also I was laid hold of by Christ Jesus. Brethren, I do not regard myself as having laid hold of it yet; but one thing I do: forgetting what lies behind and reaching forward to what lies ahead, I press on toward the goal for the prize of the upward call of God in Christ Jesus.

Like Paul, our focus needs to be on what lies ahead: our inheritance in Jesus. In order to gain our inheritance in Christ, we need to set our hearts, minds and time on Him, counting everything else as nothing and resolving that Jesus would be our All in all. We need to give ourselves to knowing Jesus at any cost, for the value of knowing Him surpasses everything else in life. He is the ultimate prize. He has taken hold of us that we might take hold of Him and become one with Christ in His resurrection life and glory.

Like Paul, as we begin to possess the different aspects of our inheritance, we will find there is always more still to experience. God's word is eternally true, so no matter what stage of spiritual growth we are at, we will always be unable to comprehend what God still has prepared for us. Our inheritance is limitless and it is always better than we could imagine. So where do we begin? How do we start entering into the reality of our inheritance?

Access by Faith

Romans 3:23-24

...for all have sinned and fall short of the glory of
God, being justified as a gift by His grace through
the redemption which is in Christ Jesus...

Justification is a gift which we experience through Jesus. Like
justification, every aspect of our inheritance in Christ is a gift
given entirely by grace. There is nothing we could ever say or
do that would make us deserving of the riches that God offers
us. It is God's grace and His grace alone. Our part is simply to
reach out and take hold of the grace of God.

Romans 5:1-2 (NKJV emphasis added)

Therefore, having been justified by faith, we have
peace with God through our Lord Jesus Christ,
through whom also we **have access by faith into
this grace** in which we stand, and rejoice in hope
of the glory of God.

Our inheritance is a gift of grace and faith accesses grace. Thus
we experience the reality of our inheritance in Christ by faith.

To gain access to something means that it has been
unlocked and is now open and available to us. Access leads to
experience. For example, to gain access to a locked car we
need a key. By using the key we can enter into the car and
experience the reality of driving. The car and all its power
become available to us once we possess the key and we know

how to use it. In the same way, faith is the key to accessing the grace of God and experiencing the different dimensions of our inheritance in Christ. We simply need to learn the way of faith.

Effective through Faith

Romans 3:21-25 (NRSV, emphasis added)
But now, irrespective of law, the righteousness of God has been disclosed, and is attested by the law and the prophets, the righteousness of God through faith in Jesus Christ for all who believe. For there is no distinction, since all have sinned and fall short of the glory of God; they are now justified by his grace as a gift, through the redemption that is in Christ Jesus, whom God put forward as a sacrifice of atonement by his blood, **effective through faith**. He did this to show his righteousness, because in his divine forbearance he had passed over the sins previously committed...

God has set before all people the gift of redemption through the blood of Christ. This gift is received by simply believing and having faith in Jesus. In fact, the sacrifice of Christ to restore people to God can be received no other way but by faith. It is only by faith that the work of the cross is made effective in our lives.

Thus faith is the only way to enter into the reality of redemption. If we have faith, we can experience redemption through Christ. Then, once we have entered into redemption, we are given the right to our awesome inheritance in Jesus. As God's children, we have the promise of our potential life in union with Him. Yet at the beginning, our potential life is simply that: a potential life. For our inheritance to become our reality, we need to possess it through experience.

According to the ways of God, we assert our right to our inheritance *through faith*. God has given us all things by grace and grace is accessed by faith. Faith is the key to reality.

Summary

Through the death of Jesus, God gave an awesome inheritance to everyone who believes in His Son. This inheritance of God, life beyond our comprehension, has been given to us. It is ours, and we own it. Yet without possession, this inheritance is of no value in our lives. As such, we need to give ourselves to living in the reality of the life that God has given us. We need to enter into and possess our inheritance in Christ. And the only way to access our inheritance is by faith. Faith is the foundation and key to living in reality.

Questions

What is my inheritance in Christ?

What is the reality that I am living in?

What is faith?

Study 12

APRIL 14, 2014

Faith and Reality

And Jesus answered saying to them, "Have faith in God."
Mark 11:22

Our inheritance is a gift, given by God's grace. The only way to access grace is by faith. Faith is the key to experiencing and possessing our inheritance in Christ. So what is faith?

Foundation for Reality

Hebrews 11:1
Now faith is the assurance of things hoped for, the conviction of things not seen.

Substance: _hupostasis_
A setting or placing under (thing put under, substructure, foundation); that which has foundation, is firm (that which has actual existence).

Faith is the substance of things hoped for, the evidence of things not seen. The Greek word *hupostasis* (substance or assurance) has the meaning of setting a place for something in the sense of providing a foundation or substructure. Faith is the foundation upon which the things we hope for come into reality. It is the basis for the various aspects of our inheritance in Christ to become our possession in actual experience. But just what is faith?

Faith: *pistis*
Conviction of the truth; derived from peitho, meaning to have confidence, be persuaded.

In Scripture, the word *faith* is used in several ways. At times it refers to the group of beliefs that shape our relationship with God. At other times it is used to refer to a person's conviction of the truth. However, when we look at the root word (*peitho*), from which the word faith is derived (*pistis),* we find that in simple terms, faith is confidence in God.[1] We believe that what He says is true and that He will do it.

With the Heart

Romans 10:8-10 (emphasis added)
But what does it say? "The word is near you, in your mouth and in your heart"—that is, the word of faith which we are preaching, that if you confess with your mouth Jesus as Lord, and believe in your heart that God raised Him from

the dead, you will be saved; **for with the heart a person believes**, resulting in righteousness, and with the mouth he confesses, resulting in salvation.

In this passage we see that those who are saved are those who believe in their hearts, *for with the heart a person believes*. Real belief is of the heart, not the mind.

In verse ten, the word translated as *believes* is the Greek word *pisteuo*, which is derived from the word *pistis*, meaning faith. In this sense, believing in God is simply having faith in Him.

So just like belief, true faith is of the heart. It is the deep confidence in our hearts that shapes our thoughts, character and behavior. In the heart we have faith and from the heart we are changed.

Belief of the Mind

expectantly
unspeakable Gift

Intellectual belief is the persuasion of our minds that comes from choosing to accept a certain doctrine or teaching as true. It is independent from experience and being based in our minds, it is essentially a philosophy. This belief comes from ourselves in the sense that we choose to believe what seems to be true. We believe in our minds that God loves us because the Scriptures say so. In our minds we can believe in love, but this intellectual belief is not the means by which the truth of God's love becomes a reality in our lives. It is with the heart that we believe and with the heart we experience reality.

Belief of the Heart

True faith is of the heart. As we saw in the *Spirit and Reality* study, the heart is often used to refer to the reality that we experience. When a person says "I know it in my head, but not in my heart" they are really saying "I believe it with my mind, but I am not experiencing the reality in my life. I know the theory, but not the experience." This is the precise difference between the belief of the mind and the faith of the heart.

The mind is the center of reason and logic and is the place of our ideas, thoughts, mindsets and concepts of God. In contrast, the heart is the center of our spiritual experience and reality. It is the place where we encounter God and receive true confidence in Him. With our minds we believe God is love, but with our hearts we experience His love. In our minds we know the theory, but in our hearts we experience reality.

Thus the faith that accesses grace and reality is faith of the heart. As we have this faith, the confidence and certainty of our heart will shape the thoughts and beliefs of our mind.

Receiving the Gift

Hebrews 4:1-2

Therefore, let us fear if, while a promise remains of entering His rest, any one of you may seem to have come short of it. For indeed we have had good news preached to us, just as they also; but the word they heard did not profit them, because it was not united by faith in those who heard.

We have the promise of an awesome inheritance in Christ. But if the word of our inheritance only gives us a head-knowledge of the truth then it has no value. The belief of our minds needs to be united by the faith of our hearts. So when we hear God speak, we need to ask the Spirit to establish His truth deep in our hearts that it may be united with real faith.

Fear, Doubt and Unbelief

James 1:6-8
But he must ask in faith without any doubting, for the one who doubts is like the surf of the sea, driven and tossed by the wind. For that man ought not to expect that he will receive anything from the Lord, being a double-minded man, unstable in all his ways.

Hebrews 3:18-19
And to whom did He swear that they would not enter His rest, but to those who were disobedient? So we see that they were not able to enter because of unbelief.

Mark 11:20-23
As they were passing by in the morning, they saw the fig tree withered from the roots up. Being reminded, Peter said to Him, "Rabbi, look, the fig tree which You cursed has withered." And Jesus answered saying to them, "Have faith in God.

Truly I say to you, whoever says to this mountain,
'Be taken up and cast into the sea,' and does not
doubt in his heart, but believes that what he says
is going to happen, it will be granted him."

To live in true faith we must overcome fear, doubt and unbelief. *Whoever does not doubt in his heart.* Just like faith, fear, doubt and unbelief reside in the heart more than the mind. They undermine our confidence in God and so prevent us from experiencing the reality of our inheritance. Because they are of the heart, we cannot overcome them by our own will-power. So instead of striving intellectually to overcome doubt by convincing ourselves that the truth is true, we simply need to seek God to remove the doubt from our hearts. Only as He releases the power of His Spirit into our hearts and dissolves the fear, doubt and unbelief, can we be free to live in real faith.

Summary

With the heart a person believes. Faith is not an intellectual belief or philosophy; it is the deep confidence of the heart. This is the faith that accesses grace and leads us to experience our inheritance. But just as faith is of the heart, so fear, doubt and unbelief are also of the heart. Thus we need God to fill us with His Spirit and love and cast out our fear and doubt, that we may have faith in Him.[2] As we have the real faith of the heart, it will access God's grace and take us into the reality of our inheritance in Jesus.

Questions

Is my faith in my heart or my mind?   *Both*

How do I move from head-belief into heart-belief?

How can I have/get more faith to experience more of my inheritance?

Rewarder of those who believe God exists and who diligently seek Him.

Study 13

April 28, 2014

Source of Faith

Now flee from youthful lusts and pursue righteousness, faith, love and peace, with those who call on the Lord from a pure heart.

2 Timothy 2:22

In Christ we are called to pursue righteousness, faith, love and peace. Like Timothy, regardless of our spiritual maturity, we are called to continually pursue more faith.[1] But how do we pursue faith? Where does faith come from?

Rev 5

Ephesians 6:23
Peace be to the brethren, and love with faith, from God the Father and the Lord Jesus Christ.

Just as God is the source of all righteousness, peace and love, so He is also the source of true faith. Faith is a gift of God. Thus our call to pursue faith is a call to continually seek God for the grace of faith.

vs good intentions personal resolutions

93

Author of Our Faith

[handwritten: See Ch 11 old Test. Faith chapter Seen from afar]

Hebrews 12:1-2

Therefore, since we have so great a cloud of witnesses surrounding us, let us also lay aside every encumbrance and the sin which so easily entangles us, and let us run with endurance the race that is set before us, fixing our eyes on Jesus, the author and perfecter of faith, who for the joy set before Him endured the cross, despising the shame, and has sat down at the right hand of the throne of God.

Jesus is the author and source of our faith. He is also the finisher and goal of faith. In Him our faith begins and ends; our confidence flows from Christ and leads us back to Him.

[handwritten: needs + make Connections + participate]

Ephesians 2:8-9

For by grace you have been saved through faith; and that not of yourselves, it is the gift of God; not as a result of works, so that no one may boast.

The gifts of God cannot be earned by striving or works. Just as we are unable to create true joy or peace by our own efforts, so we cannot create real faith by ourselves. Thus our call is not to try and create faith in our hearts, but to pursue the gift of faith by taking hold of God's constant grace. As we are obedient to pursue more faith, the Spirit will form new confidence in our hearts. So how does God create more faith in us?

Faith from Hearing

Romans 10:17

So faith comes from hearing, and hearing by the word [*rhema*] of Christ.

The word *rhema* means a spoken word from the living voice. The *rhema* of God is the sound of His living voice speaking to us. Thus faith comes by hearing the voice of God. God speaks and creates faith in us. He gives us the deep confidence that knows beyond any doubt that God will fulfill His word to us.

To know God's voice we need the Spirit to teach us how to listen and hear. It is the role of the Spirit to lead us into truth and so as we join with Him, He will lead us into the reality of hearing His voice.

John 18:37

Therefore Pilate said to Him, "So You are a king?" Jesus answered, "You say correctly that I am a king. For this I have been born, and for this I have come into the world, to testify to the truth. Everyone who is of the truth hears My voice."

Everyone who is of the truth hears Christ's voice. When we give ourselves to living in the truth, we will hear Jesus' voice. It is a promise of God that He will fulfill: we will hear His voice. As we continue to hear the Spirit speak to us, He will continue to create faith in our hearts. This faith will then let us access God's grace and experience more of our inheritance in Christ.

Confirming His Voice

2 Corinthians 13:1
This is the third time I am coming to you. Every fact [*rhema*] is to be confirmed by the testimony of two or three witnesses.

Earlier we learned that every *rhema* is confirmed by two or three witnesses. When God speaks to us, He will confirm the word He has spoken.[2] This confirmation gives us certainty in hearing God and provides a firm foundation for unyielding faith and confidence in Him. Knowing that God has spoken, we can be sure that God will fulfill His word to us. As He has spoken so it shall come to pass.[3] He will make it happen.

Witness of Spirit and Word

Romans 8:16-17 (NKJV)
The Spirit Himself bears witness with our spirit that we are children of God, and if children, then heirs—heirs of God and joint heirs with Christ, if indeed we suffer with Him, that we may also be glorified together.

The Spirit of God in us bears witness that we are children and heirs of God. The Spirit is a witness to the truth. He is the source of our discernment. So as we abide in the Spirit, He will witness to the truth of His voice. If our hearts are right but we are mishearing God, He will correct us. In this way, we can look to the Spirit to confirm the words we hear.

The word of God also confirms the voice of God. When we hear God speak, His words will always be consistent with the overall tenor of Scripture.[4] God's word is the standard of truth which He will not contradict. Thus to grow in hearing God, we need to become people who love the truth and abide in His word. We need to continually seek God to open our hearts and minds that we may come to know more of the message and heart of Scripture.

As we receive the witness of the Spirit and use Scripture as our basis for truth, we start to become people of the truth. We become people who hear His voice, receive His faith and live in reality.

Crying Out

Luke 18:35-40

As Jesus was approaching Jericho, a blind man was sitting by the road begging. Now hearing a crowd going by, he began to inquire what this was. They told him that Jesus of Nazareth was passing by. And he called out, saying, "Jesus, Son of David, have mercy on me!" Those who led the way were sternly telling him to be quiet; but he kept crying out all the more, "Son of David, have mercy on me!" And Jesus stopped and commanded that he be brought to Him; and when he came near, He questioned him, "What do you want Me to do for you?"

Faith is a gift from God that is only available through Jesus. Thus if we want to have more faith then we need the Spirit of God to create faith in us. We can trust in Him with our minds, but unless He acts, we cannot experience Him in our hearts. As such, we are called to actively pursue the grace of faith.

All we can do to receive this faith is cry out to God. Like the disciples in the storm, we know that if Jesus does not come and speak to us, we will surely die. Like the blind man by the road, all we can do is keep calling out to the One who can save us. In both of these cases Jesus was passing by, but was stopped by the cry of desperate people. In the same way, we need to be desperate for faith and reality. We need to ask, seek, knock, call, wait and listen for Him. We need to continue to cry out for faith, that we may know more of the reality of Jesus. If we possess this overwhelming need for Jesus, we can be sure that He will stop and act. He will give us the faith we so desperately long for.

Summary

Jesus is the source, sustainer and finisher of our faith. Our faith comes from Jesus and leads us straight back to Him. He is our beginning, middle and end.

Like all the other qualities of God, faith of the heart is a gift of His grace. We cannot earn faith; rather we can only seek God to give us the true confidence which is faith. And He will. When we cry out to Jesus, He will not disappoint us. He will speak to us and create in our hearts the faith we need to possess more of our inheritance in Christ.

Questions

How have I heard God speak lately?

Have I received His faith?

Do I want to hear God more?

meek bele day
may 20   /1 9am

Study 14

Enoch + Elijah pleased God

May 5, 2014

Living Faith

By faith Abraham, when he was called, obeyed by going out to a place which he was to receive for an inheritance...

Hebrews 11:8

(Faith is a gift of grace that is formed within us as God speaks.) It is the deep confidence of the heart that comes with knowing that God will fulfill His word in us. This is the confidence that accesses the grace of God and lets us experience the reality of our inheritance in Christ.

given + received

Living Faith

2 Corinthians 4:13-14

But having the same spirit of faith, according to what is written, "I believed, therefore I spoke," we also believe, therefore we also speak, knowing that He who raised the Lord Jesus will raise us also with Jesus and will present us with you.

When we have the confidence of faith, what we believe will be naturally expressed in our words. In the *Word of Power* study we saw how the voice of God is powerful and creative. He speaks and it is done. In the same way, when God creates faith in us and leads us to speak out in faith, what we say will also be powerful and creative. When our faith is sourced in God, the words of faith we speak will release the power of the Spirit to bring those words into being. In this way, God will speak through us, and it will be done.

> **James 2:14-17**
> What use is it, my brethren, if someone says he has faith but he has no works? Can that faith save him? If a brother or sister is without clothing and in need of daily food, and one of you says to them, "Go in peace, be warmed and be filled," and yet you do not give them what is necessary for their body, what use is that? Even so faith, if it has no works, is dead, being by itself.

Faith needs expression to live. Just as true faith compels us to speak, it also compels us to act. Our inner confidence flows through our outward behavior. And like our words, when our actions are expressions of our faith, they will be powerful in the spirit.

Faith and Obedience

John 9:1-7

As He passed by, He saw a man blind from birth.
And His disciples asked Him, "Rabbi, who sinned,
this man or his parents, that he would be born
blind?" Jesus answered, "It was neither that this
man sinned, nor his parents; but it was so that the
works of God might be displayed in him. We
must work the works of Him who sent Me as long
as it is day; night is coming when no one can
work. While I am in the world, I am the Light of
the world." When He had said this, He spat on
the ground, and made clay of the spittle, and
applied the clay to his eyes, and said to him, "Go,
wash in the pool of Siloam" (which is translated,
Sent). So he went away and washed, and came
back seeing.

In this passage, the blind man was healed only after he had
obeyed Jesus. In Scripture, people were often healed instantly
by God, yet this man only received his sight once he had acted
in faith and obedience. His actions completed his faith, which
accessed the grace of God's healing.

James 2:22

You see that faith was working with his works,
and as a result of the works, faith was perfected...

Like the blind man, as we grow in Christ, we will also have times when our faith needs perfecting through our actions or words. At these times, we simply need to act in obedience and confidence. When the words and works that we say and do are expressions of our faith, they will be spiritually powerful. In themselves they carry no power of their own, but because they flow from faith, they carry the power of the Spirit of God. Thus as our inner confidence is perfected by our outward acts, we access grace, release power, and experience reality.

Desire and Obedience

> **Isaiah 1:19**
> "If you consent and obey, you will eat the best of the land; but if you refuse and rebel, you will be devoured by the sword." Truly, the mouth of the LORD has spoken.

For Israel, the land was their inheritance given to them by God. Here God tells Israel that if they consent and obey they will eat the best of the land. In this passage, the word *consent* means to desire and be willing.¹ The principle we find here also applies to us: if we desire God and obey His voice, we will possess the best of our inheritance. This is an awesome promise of God: we can have the very best of our inheritance in Jesus. To take hold of this promise we need to add desire and obedience to our faith. But how do we build more desire for Jesus? Where can we find the inner strength to obey God?

God at Work

Philippians 2:13

...for it is God who is at work in you, both to will and to work for His good pleasure.

God works in us to will and to work for His pleasure. In other words, the Spirit of God wants to form in us the desire for Jesus and the strength and resolve to obey Him.

Thus, if we want the will and power to obey God, then we can call on Him to give us real desire and an obedient heart. As we seek God and work with Him to fulfill this word in us, we will start to desire Christ and genuinely want what He wants. As He changes our hearts, it will become increasingly natural for us to live and act in obedience to His perfect will.

So what is God's will for us? God's will is His love. His will is that we would enter into and possess the fullness of our inheritance in Christ. His will is that His love would define us; that we would love Him with all our hearts and love others and ourselves. His will is that we would have abundant life in Christ, being fruitful in every aspect of Jesus. His will is that we would become our true selves, people who reflect the nature and love of God. His will is that we would be one with Christ. It is this will He calls and empowers us to obey.

So if we honestly call on God to do His work in us, He will create true desire and a spirit of obedience within us, and we will eat the best of the Land. It is a promise. He will make it happen. We simply have to ask, receive and act.

Building Faith and Desire

Jude 20-21 (NRSV)
But you, beloved, build yourselves up on your most holy faith; pray in the Holy Spirit; keep yourselves in the love of God; look forward to the mercy of our Lord Jesus Christ that leads to eternal life.

Faith is living and progressive; it grows and deepens. As such, we are called to continually build ourselves up in our faith. To grow in confidence we need to hear God's voice, pray in the Spirit and abide in His love.

Mark 5:36b
"Do not be afraid any longer, only believe."

To grow in faith, we also need to rid ourselves of fear, doubt, unbelief, fantasy and ignorance. To do this, we need to see the presence of these things in our hearts as the start of sin.[2] We can then repent and seek God's forgiveness and cleansing from fear and doubt that we might receive more of His faith.

In the same way, to.grow in desire and obedience, we need to let God free us from all those things that undermine our love for Jesus and our motivation to obey Him. We need to resist apathy, indifference, and complacency. We need to seek God to give us faithful hearts that love and desire Him above all else. Then as Jesus becomes our hearts' desire, our resolve to obey Him will become a natural part of who we are.

Summary

Our only way to experience grace and reality is through faith in Jesus. This faith is the gift of deep confidence of our hearts that comes as we hear God speak to us. It is a confidence that lives through our words and actions. As we continue to build a living faith and combine it with deep desire and obedience, we have the promise that God will lead us into the best of our inheritance.

Jesus is the creator of our faith and He is also the creator of our desire. He works in us to desire Him and to act in His love. Thus in Jesus we have everything we need to experience the life He has called us to. He has made it all possible. We simply need to give ourselves to His will and call on God to do His work in us. As the Spirit creates more desire and faith in us, we can perfect our faith with actions and experience more of the grace and love of God in Jesus.

Questions

Am I speaking and living out my faith?   *yes*

Do I want the desire to obey?   *yes*

How can I increase my faith and desire?   *trusting*
Loving others
Doing good
Blessing others
Praying constantly.

Study 15

may 12, 2014

ϙ

☧

active

Faith and Maturity

+

⤴

For whatever is born of God overcomes the world; and this is the
victory that has overcome the world—our faith.

1 John 5:4

It can be natural for us to listen for God's voice when we are faced with outward challenges or decisions. Yet often we can overlook the role of God's voice in guiding our inner growth and direction. We assume that spiritual maturity will simply come with the passing of time. However, this is not the case.

On to Maturity

Hebrews 5:11-6:2

Concerning him we have much to say, and it is hard to explain, since you have become dull of hearing. For though by this time you ought to be teachers, you have need again for someone to teach you the elementary principles of the oracles of God, and you have come to need milk and not solid food. For everyone who partakes only of milk is not accustomed to the word of righteousness, for he is an infant. But solid food is for the mature, who because of practice have their senses trained to discern good and evil.

Therefore leaving the elementary teaching about the Christ, let us press on to maturity, not laying again a foundation of repentance from dead works and of faith toward God, of instruction about washings and laying on of hands, and the resurrection of the dead and eternal judgment.

The passing of time brings physical maturity. Babies grow into children who then grow into adults. However this is not always true for spiritual growth. In this passage we see that while the people should have grown to become teachers, they were still spiritual infants. They were dull and unable to receive more truth because they had not been active in their spiritual growth.[1] They had failed to mature. The message for us is clear: let us press on to maturity in Christ.[2]

Inheritance and Maturity

Change is a defining feature of growth. Therefore our call to spiritual maturity is a call to spiritual change. Such change is found in Jesus. He is the one who transforms us within and leads us to possess more of our inheritance.

When Jesus leads us to experience a part of our inheritance, we can mature spiritually as we let that experience change us. For example, when the Spirit takes us into joy, we feel joy. But feelings fade. For our experience of joy to produce lasting growth, we need to let it change us. We need to let the joy of God heal, soften and strengthen us. We need to let it penetrate our hearts and change our inner nature. We need His joy to live and remain in us.

Colossians 3:9-11

Do not lie to one another, since you laid aside the old self with its evil practices, and have put on the new self who is being renewed to a true knowledge according to the image of the One who created him—a renewal in which there is no distinction between Greek and Jew, circumcised and uncircumcised, barbarian, Scythian, slave and freeman, but Christ is all, and in all.

We are called to put on our new self, made in the image of Jesus. This verse is a call to transformation. Thus the purpose of entering our inheritance is not just to experience Jesus, but to be renewed and transformed by Him. This is the way to maturity. It is to continually enter into more of our inheritance in Christ, being continually conformed to our true nature or self. In this sense, spiritual maturity is simply returning to God's original design for us. It is growing in love and unity with Him.

Step by Step

Faith is the key to our maturity and transformation. Our faith starts and ends with Jesus. As such, to grow spiritually we need to focus on Jesus and listen to Him regarding the next step into our inheritance.

If we set our focus on particular aspects of our inheritance and not on Jesus, then we risk getting out of step with the Spirit. When we get out of step, we try to progress in God on our terms and in our own strength. For example, healing is a part of our inheritance. Jesus died for our healing.[3] However, if we want healing more than God's present will for us, then we can start trying to make it happen. We believe harder for our healing. We try to build faith by reading Scriptures of healing. We command our healing. We declare it and we sing of it, yet we fail to listen to God to see if He is actually healing us now. When this happens we disconnect our faith from God and His will for us now. We make the faith something of us and our determination, rather than of God and His power.

Faith will always be a gift from God that comes through hearing Him. Our best efforts to believe cannot produce the real faith that accesses grace and reality. Only God can lead us into transformation. This reflects a fundamental truth of the gospel: that it is not by our works that we reach God, rather it is only by His work that we can experience and know Him. This is the gospel of grace and it is true for faith. The deep and abiding confidence of the heart, which is true faith, comes from God alone by His grace.

From Faith to Faith

Thus our spiritual journey is a walk of faith, made up of a series of confident steps and quiet transformations. As such, faith is the key to growing in God. If we are to press on to maturity in Christ then we need to pursue the grace of faith.

As we seek God for more faith, the Spirit will speak to us and create new confidence in our hearts. Our faith will then naturally access grace and lead us to experience new aspects of our inheritance. Thus to keep growing in Christ we need to continue to hear Him speak and have confidence in His voice. We need to live by faith.[4]

> **Romans 1:16-17**
> For I am not ashamed of the gospel, for it is the power of God for salvation to everyone who believes, to the Jew first and also to the Greek. For in it the righteousness of God is revealed from faith to faith; as it is written, "but the righteous man shall live by faith."

The faith that leads to righteousness is not just a one-time act of believing at the point of conversion. We are not righteous simply because we once had confidence in Christ. Rather, the righteous one shall *live* by faith.

We live only in the present moment and so to live by faith is to have confidence now, at this present time. Thus, to grow in Christ we need to pursue a present faith. What is the Spirit saying to us now? What is He leading us into today?

Faith and Patience

Hebrews 6:11-12

And we desire that each one of you show the same diligence so as to realize the full assurance of hope until the end, so that you will not be sluggish, but imitators of those who through faith and patience inherit the promises.

To experience more of our inheritance in Christ, we need to live each day in the faith God gives. But what if God speaks to us and His word is not fulfilled straight away?

We should not be discouraged by any delay of the reality: delay is not denial. It is by faith and patience that we inherit the promises. The word that God speaks is true and it will come to pass, for as Scripture says: God's word shall not return void, but will accomplish its purpose.[5] Often it will be immediate, but sometimes God's timing or fulfillment may not be quite as we expect. This is okay; God's timing and ways are perfect. He is not slow in keeping His promises and what He has spoken will be fulfilled.[6] Our part is to stand firm in faith and obedience.

Summary

In the physical realm, maturity comes with the passage of time. However, it is not always true that we mature spiritually as we physically age. To grow spiritually we need to be active in our growth and learn to live by faith. We need to combine a present faith with desire and obedience to the voice of Jesus.

Jesus will lead us into the riches of our inheritance in His perfect timing. So when the Spirit speaks to us, we can stand firm in faith and patience, knowing that He will bring His word to pass and we will inherit the promise. It will happen.

As we enter into new aspects of our inheritance by faith, our experiences of God can lead to lasting change. If we are willing, the Spirit can establish our inheritance in our hearts and transform us into our true selves. Through faith and grace we can become the people we were always designed to be: people who are created in the image of God to live in love and unity with Him.

Bottom line for the study.

Questions

Have I been active or passive in my spiritual growth?
Have my experiences of God produced lasting change? *yes*
What is my next step of faith?

today joy peace gentleness
focus
Hunger for Gods word
through Jesus
Be active by faith
Learn to live by faith
patience
inheritance grace
+ glory
Amen

show you
make you
bless you
make great your name
shall be a blessing
blessed are the blessers
cursed are the cursers
families of the earth blessed

Study 16

may 19, 2014

The Promised Land

Then it shall be, when you enter the land which the LORD your God gives you as an inheritance, and you possess it and live in it...

Deuteronomy 26:1

Knowing that we have an inheritance in Christ beyond our comprehension, we are called to enter into, possess and live in the reality of our inheritance. As a summary of *Series One*, we will look at Israel's inheritance in the Promised Land.

Truth and Reality

The gift of the Promised Land begins with Abraham.

> **Genesis 12:1-3**
> Now the LORD said to Abram, "Go forth from your country, and from your relatives and from your father's house, to the land which I will show you; and I will make you a great nation, and I will

117

bless you, and make your name great; and so you shall be a blessing; and I will bless those who bless you, and the one who curses you I will curse. And in you all the families of the earth will be blessed."

Genesis 17:7-8

"I will establish My covenant between Me and you and your descendants after you throughout their generations for an everlasting covenant, to be God to you and to your descendants after you. I will give to you and to your descendants after you, the land of your sojournings, all the land of Canaan, for an everlasting possession; and I will be their God."

God called Abraham into a covenant relationship and gave Him a promise of great life and blessing. To enter into the blessing, Abraham had to act in faith by leaving his homeland and going to live in the promised land of Canaan. Abraham believed God and obeyed.

Abraham's relationship with God was connected to the land of Canaan. The land represented the fulfillment of God's promise to Abraham, and dwelling in the land reflected Abraham's faith and obedience in God.

The land was a gift that was given to Abraham and his descendants. So like Abraham, Israel's possession of land and their fruitfulness in it reflected their relationship with God.

When the nation lived righteously before God they possessed the land and prospered. When they rebelled against God they lost possession of the land with their exile mirroring their disconnection from God.[1] Thus obedience led to possession and fruitfulness, however rebellion led to poverty and loss.

Our Reality

In a spiritual sense, the Promised Land represents the reality of our relationship with God. Just as Abraham was called to live in a new land, so Jesus calls us to know Him as our new life. He is our inheritance.

The land was given to Abraham as a gift of love, entirely unearned in any way. In the same way, we cannot earn a relationship with God. He has offered it to us purely as a gift of love. As with all the gifts of God, the only way to receive our inheritance is through faith. So like Abraham, to enter into the reality of our inheritance, we need to have confidence in God's promise and be obedient to His voice.

The Promised Land

Abraham was the father of Isaac, who was the father of Jacob. Jacob and His sons' families left Canaan to escape a famine and resettled in Egypt. A new king then came to power and enslaved God's people. After a time, God sent Moses and freed His people. They fled Egypt and followed God into the wilderness of Sinai as they travelled back towards their inheritance in Canaan. While in the wilderness, God spoke to Israel of the Promised Land.

Deuteronomy 8:1-10
"Therefore, you shall keep the commandments of
the LORD your God, to walk in His ways and to
fear Him. For the LORD your God is bringing you
into a good land, a land of brooks of water, of
fountains and springs, flowing forth in valleys
and hills; a land of wheat and barley, of vines and
fig trees and pomegranates, a land of olive oil and
honey; a land where you will eat food without
scarcity, in which you will not lack anything; a
land whose stones are iron, and out of whose hills
you can dig copper. When you have eaten and are
satisfied, you shall bless the LORD your God for
the good land which He has given you."

God set the Promised Land before the Israelites as an
inheritance of abundant life and richness. In the same way, He
has set before us an awesome inheritance in Christ: a life of
spiritual abundance in unity with Jesus.

All the dimensions of relationship with God, all the aspects
of Jesus' nature, power and life, have been given to us to enter
into and possess. They are our inheritance. Yet, just like Israel
in the wilderness, having an inheritance of surpassing wealth
is of no value to us if we fail to experience that wealth. Thus to
possess the abundant life that God has for us, we need to
pursue the reality that comes by faith. We need to seek the
Spirit of God to give us His grace and faith that we might
possess the land of our inheritance.

Little by Little

Deuteronomy 7:22

"The LORD your God will clear away these
nations before you little by little; you will not be
able to put an end to them quickly, for the wild
beasts would grow too numerous for you."

God led His people to take the land little by little, nation by
nation. He did this so that Israel would completely secure
their inheritance and be fruitful in the land.[2]

2 Corinthians 3:18

But we all, with unveiled face, beholding as in a
mirror the glory of the Lord, are being
transformed into the same image from glory to
glory, just as from the Lord, the Spirit.

God's pattern of possession also applies to our spiritual
growth. We take it step by step, from glory to glory. We do
not receive our full inheritance or complete transformation
when we first believe. Rather we are changed by degrees of
glory into people who live in love and unity with Jesus.

At some stages in our journey we may need to overcome
the forces of greed, lust, pride or doubt in our hearts. At other
times we may receive the love, faith, joy or peace of God.
Regardless of what God is doing, our call is to take it little by
little, without getting stressed over the things we have yet to
conquer or receive. We simply take the next step of faith.

Led by the Spirit

Deuteronomy 20:1-4

"When you go out to battle against your enemies and see horses and chariots and people more numerous than you, do not be afraid of them; for the LORD your God, who brought you up from the land of Egypt, is with you. When you are approaching the battle, the priest shall come near and speak to the people. He shall say to them, 'Hear, O Israel, you are approaching the battle against your enemies today. Do not be fainthearted. Do not be afraid, or panic, or tremble before them, for the LORD your God is the one who goes with you, to fight for you against your enemies, to save you.'"

In this passage, God gives Israel the promise that He Himself would fight for the Israelites. In terms of taking our spiritual inheritance this is an important principle: the only battles we can win are those that God is fighting. Thus we need to focus on what God is doing in us at the present time.

For example, regardless of how much we may want to possess His gifts, if God is currently calling us to fight and overcome our insecurity, then this is what we need to set our focus on. This is where we will find the grace and faith to overcome. He will give us His gifts in His perfect time. Our part is simply to listen to Him and let Him lead us in what He is doing now.

The Living Word

Deuteronomy 1:21

"See, the LORD your God has placed the land before you; go up, take possession, as the LORD, the God of your fathers, has spoken to you. Do not fear or be dismayed."

God spoke clearly to Israel about taking the Promised Land. His word was His *rhema* to Israel; it was the spoken, powerful and living word of God. When God spoke, the power of His Spirit was released to perform that word. If Israel received the word with a heart of faith, it would be done. God would fulfill His word.

Like Israel, we need to hear God's voice. We need to let the Spirit breathe life into His word that it may become the living word or *rhema* of God to us.

Hebrews 4:2

For indeed we have had good news preached to us, just as they also; but the word they heard did not profit them, because it was not united by faith in those who heard.

For the word of God to be profitable in us, we need to have faith. When God speaks, we need to seek Him to create real confidence in our hearts. As He forms His confidence in us, we will access His grace and experience the reality of His word. Our inheritance will become our possession.

Faith and Obedience

Israel took their inheritance little by little, city by city. As God took them into the land, the Spirit showed them how they were to take each city. Thus to possess their inheritance in God, the Israelites simply had to hear God and act in faith and obedience. He would do the rest.

Joshua 6:1-5, 20

Now Jericho was tightly shut because of the sons of Israel; no one went out and no one came in. The LORD said to Joshua, "See, I have given Jericho into your hand, with its king and the valiant warriors. You shall march around the city, all the men of war circling the city once. You shall do so for six days. Also seven priests shall carry seven trumpets of rams' horns before the ark; then on the seventh day you shall march around the city seven times, and the priests shall blow the trumpets. It shall be that when they make a long blast with the ram's horn, and when you hear the sound of the trumpet, all the people shall shout with a great shout; and the wall of the city will fall down flat, and the people will go up every man straight ahead."

...So the people shouted, and priests blew the trumpets; and when the people heard the sound of the trumpet, the people shouted with a great shout and the wall fell down flat, so that the people went up into the city, every man straight ahead, and they took the city.

Jericho was the first city taken by Israel as their inheritance. To possess Jericho, Israel followed God's command exactly. They marched around the city for six days and on the seventh day, after marching around the city seven times, they blew their trumpets, gave a shout, and the walls came down. God spoke His word, Israel heard, believed and obeyed. Their confidence was perfected through their actions and words, and so it was through their living faith that Israel secured the victory.[3]

The principles revealed in the taking of the Promised Land are the same for us as we enter into our new life in Christ. To possess our inheritance we need to hear God speak and have complete confidence in His word. Like Israel at Jericho, often God may call us to act in faith before He leads us into the reality of a particular aspect of our inheritance. When we obey the call of the Spirit to speak and act in faith, we access God's grace and release His power to bring about the victory within us.

Summary

Reality is found in Jesus. He is the ultimate truth and reality. God's word reveals the truth of Jesus and the life we can have in union with Him. However apart from the Spirit, the word of God can only give us intellectual knowledge. To experience Jesus we need the theory of the word to become our reality.

The Spirit and the word work together to lead us into reality. As the Spirit breathes into the word, it becomes the living and active word of God. This is our *rhema*—the direct and living voice of God to us.

Faith comes by hearing the living voice of God. Thus when the Spirit speaks to us, He creates real faith in us. This faith is the deep, abiding confidence of the heart. It is the certainty that God will perform His word and it will come to pass in our lives. And it does. As we follow God in faith with a heart of desire and a spirit of obedience, His word is fulfilled in us and we enter into more of our spiritual inheritance in Jesus.

> **Deuteronomy 30:19-20**
> "I call heaven and earth to witness against you today, that I have set before you life and death, the blessing and the curse. So choose life in order that you may live, you and your descendants, by loving the LORD your God, by obeying His voice, and by holding fast to Him; for this is your life and the length of your days, that you may live in the land which the LORD swore to your fathers, to Abraham, Isaac, and Jacob, to give them."

Our inheritance in Christ is more than we could possibly imagine or hope to receive. It is the life, nature and presence of Jesus. It is His life that we choose by loving and obeying God and holding fast to Him.[4] He is our Promised Land. Jesus is our inheritance that has been given to us through love and grace. The Father has prepared all this for us and it is more than we can imagine or dream. All that remains is for us to choose this life, to take His hand and let Him lead us on to experience the reality of our inheritance in Jesus Christ.

Questions

Will I choose Life today?

What is my Promised Land?

What is the next step into my inheritance?

Contact Us

Therefore encourage one another and build up one another,
just as you also are doing.
1 Thessalonians 5:11

If you would like to make contact with us, please visit our website or email us. On our website you will be able to find links to *Series Two* of the *One with Christ* series as well as other resources.

Website | www.onewithchrist.com
Email | info@onewithchrist.com

Please feel free to send through any feedback you may have on the studies. We would love to hear from you.

Reference Notes

Introduction
[1] John 6:63

1. Truth and Reality
[1] See http://strongsnumbers.com/greek/225.htm

2. Spirit and Reality
[1] 1 John 4:8, 1 John 4:16

[2] John 15:11, Psalm 16:11

[3] John 14:6, John 6:35

[4] In Scripture, the only time that the word *kardia* refers to something other than our spiritual center is in Matthew 12:40. There Jesus uses it when He speaks of the Son of Man spending "three days and three nights in the heart (*kardia*) of the earth."

[5] The word *heart* is also often used more broadly to encompass the will, emotions, passions, appetites, affections, purposes, endeavors, thoughts and character of a person; attributes which overlap with the *soul* and *mind*. However, the main point here is that the heart is the center of spiritual and therefore eternal experience.

[6] See Proverbs 4:23. The heart is the spirit out of which the springs of life flow. It is the center of our spiritual and natural lives.

[7] See Colossians 1:16-17

[8] Philippians 1:21

3. Worship in Truth

[1] See the *Spirit and Reality* study.

[2] *WordNet: A Lexical Database for English* © 1995 George A. Miller

[3] *The American Heritage® Dictionary of the English Language, Fourth Edition.* (2003)

[4] *Merriam-Webster Online Dictionary* © 2010

[5] *Collins English Dictionary – Complete and Unabridged.* ©1991, 1994, 1998, 2000, 2003

[6] In Hebrews 12:28-29 we are called to serve God with reverence and awe. We cannot make ourselves have awe by our own efforts. All we can do is seek the Spirit to give us a revelation of the reality of God. Only when we experience a measure of the glory of God can we have a genuine sense of reverence and awe.

[7] John 17:24-26

[8] 1 John 4:8, 1 John 4:16

[9] To fully appreciate this act of worship, spend some time immersed in this Scripture. Read through it slowly, imagining the scene, the tears, the smell and the sound. Seek the Spirit to open your heart to feel the brokenness and see the depth of love in worship revealed here.

[10] Note that the word translated as *imitators* is the Greek word *mimetes*, which means to mimic or follow. This is a call to follow the example of Jesus. It is not a call to try and imitate Jesus in our own strength, but to follow Him as He leads us into the reality of living in true love, humility and worship.

[11] See 3 John 1:4

[12] Colossians 3:12, Romans 5:5

5. The Spoken Word

[1] John 14:26

[2] In this study we have focused on hearing God through His word. In *Series Three* we will cover hearing God's voice in different ways and receiving confirmation in more depth. For other resources on hearing God visit www.onewithchrist.com.

6. Word of Power

[1] Genesis 1:3

[2] Matthew 8:1-3

[3] Note that Titus 3:5-7 speaks of being washed by the Spirit of God. Thus the Holy Spirit and the word of God combine to wash us. The written word of God reveals the reality of being spiritually clean. The Holy Spirit then fulfills His word in us. He breathes His life into the word and the written word becomes the living and spoken word of God. Through the Spirit, the word of God releases the power of God to wash us and make us truly clean.

[4] Joel 2:11: Strong is He who carries out His word.

[5] Jeremiah 1:11-12: God watches over His word to perform it.
Joshua 21:45: Not one of God's promises failed.

[6] Romans 10:11: Those who believe in Him will not be disappointed.

7. Our Inheritance

[1] 1 John 4:8

[2] Psalm 16:11

[3] 1 Corinthians 6:17

8. Inheritance of Life

[1] 1 Peter 1:22-23

[2] Sermon 76, John Wesley

³ Note that it would be against the nature of God to call us to do things that are impossible. For if God gives us a command that we cannot keep then He is consigning us to a life of disobedience, which is sin. This is contrary to the nature of God, for God is love and by His power He leads us into righteousness rather than into sin. Jesus came and died to free us from sin, not to bind us in it. So to presume that there are commands in Scripture that are impossible for us to attain is to question the all-loving and all-powerful nature of God. The commands and calls in Scripture are promises of God that He can bring to pass in us. Through the indwelling life of Jesus, He can do it.

9. Inheritance and Possession

¹ Father (Romans 8:15), Mother (Luke 13:34), Brother (Matthew 12:46-50), Master (Matthew 23:8-12), Savior (1 Timothy 4:10), Judge, (2 Timothy 4:1-2), Teacher (John 13:13), Counselor (Isaiah 9:6), Shepherd (John 10:16), Helper (John 14:26), Protector (2 Samuel 22:3), Provider (Matthew 6:25-34), Lord (John 13:13), Friend (John 15:13-15), Bridegroom (John 3:28-29), Husband (Isaiah 54:5), and God (Exodus 6:7).

² John 14:16, John 14:26, John 15:26

10. Desire

¹ Ephesians 3:14-19

12. Faith and Reality   PISTIS   *a deep confidence*

¹ *Pistis* means the conviction of the truth. Conviction in this sense is simply a deep confidence. We are confident in God and we are convinced that what He says is true. However, for the purposes of this study, rather than using the term *conviction*, which can carry alternative meanings such legal judgment or correction, for clarity we will use the phrase *deep confidence*.

² 1 John 4:18

13. Source of Faith

[1] Note that Paul calls Timothy to pursue faith in 1 Timothy 6:11 and again in 2 Timothy 2:22. Paul was not denying that Timothy had faith, but rather he was encouraging Timothy not to settle for his current measure of faith. As Timothy matured in Christ, he was called to seek more and more faith. So like Timothy, if we are to continue to grow in God we also need to continually pursue more faith. See also Jude 20-21.

[2] God can speak in many different ways and will likewise confirm His voice in a variety of ways. See *Series Three* for further study on hearing God and receiving confirmation.

[3] Joel 2:11, Jeremiah 1:12, Ezekiel 24:14, Joshua 21:45 *PSALM 119:160*

[4] The sum of God's word is truth (Psalm 119:160). When taken in isolation, many verses in Scripture can seem to violate the overall tenor of the word of God. Yet when we read these verses in context, we find that all Scripture perfectly harmonizes together. Knowing this, we need to have integrity in seeking confirmation in Scripture and remain true to the whole truth of the word.

14. Living Faith

abah

[1] The word translated as *consent* is *abah,* meaning to be willing, consent, yield to, accept, or desire. *WILLING*

[2] Romans 14:23

15. Faith and Maturity *teleiotes*

[1] Melchizedek is a type of Christ and the subject of verse 11 of this passage. The words *concerning him* refer to Melchizedek.

[2] The word translated as maturity in this passage is the Greek word *teleiotes* meaning perfection. *perfection*

[3] 1 Peter 2:24, Isaiah 53:5

[4] Note that in our spiritual journey in Christ, just as we are transformed from glory to glory, so we live from faith to faith (see 2 Corinthians 3:18).

Thus as we mature in Christ, our confidence in God continually grows. As such, if we are not hearing God speak in the present time, the silence does not nullify the faith that we have already received. Rather we are to stand firm in the confidence we have received thus far and remain faithful with what God has given us. God will also remain faithful to us and in His time He will speak, give us more faith and lead us on in our journey.

⁵ Isaiah 55:11

⁶ Joshua 21:45, 23:14, Joel 2:11, Jeremiah 1:12, Ezekiel 24:14, 2 Peter 3:9

16. The Promised Land   dabaq

¹ In Scripture it is clear that the people of Israel were not entirely cut off from God when they lost possession of the land. Throughout their exile, God maintained His relationship with His people and brought about their eventual return to the Promised Land. God remained faithful, even when Israel was unfaithful. Thus rather than representing the end of Israel's relationship with God, the loss of the Promised Land reflected a degree of spiritual separation that occurred when Israel rebelled against God. The people of Israel chose to walk in their own ways and by doing so they separated themselves from God and forfeited their inheritance. That inheritance not only included all the blessings that flow from a right relationship with God, but for Israel their inheritance from God included the Promised Land. Thus in the Promised Land we learn that obedience to God brings great blessing and that rebellion brings unspeakable loss. As such, we need to learn from Israel and seek to always walk in the love and grace of God with humble and obedient hearts.

² Exodus 23:30

³ Hebrews 11:30

³ The Hebrew phrase translated as "hold fast" is *dabaq* which means to cling, adhere, cleave (together), pursue, be joined and abide fast. It is a word that is often used in the sense of unity (see Genesis 2:24).

Index of Scriptures